SUCCESS MADE SIMPLE

Achieve your business and personal dreams by mastering one new habit at a time.

MICK HAWES

2nd Edition published in 2014 by

Intertype
Unit 45, 125 Highbury Road
BURWOOD VIC 3125, Australia
© Mick Hawes 2014

National Library of Australia Cataloguing-in-Publication entry:

Author:	Hawes, Mick
Title:	Success Made Simple: Achieve your business and personal dreams by mastering one new habit at a time / Mick Hawes
ISBN:	978-0-9874466-2-6
Subjects:	Change.
	Quality of life.
	Success in business.
	Achievement motivation.
Dewey Number:	153.8

Printed in Australia by Intertype

Graphic Design by Intertype.

Disclaimer:

Contact Information

If you would like more information on the strategies, tools and techniques available to help you grow your business or you would just like to follow me on this journey:

Visit this page to access bonus content that will help you apply the concepts in the book:

http://bit.ly/1tQhLCA

Or scan this QR Code:

Or connect via my social media presence:

Facebook:	uncoverhiddenprofits
LinkedIn:	Mick Hawes
YouTube:	Mick Hawes
Google+:	Mick Hawes

I nearly made the mistake of 'I can't afford it'

"As a start-up business I nearly made the mistake of 'I can't afford it' but realised my business success depended on my mental and physical fitness. Frankly, my business wouldn't have survived the initial months, let alone thrived, without the assistance of Mick Hawes. In dollar terms the return has been tenfold. In personal terms it is immeasurable."

Helen Basset — Proprietor, Tas Tour Radio

The empowering feeling this knowledge provides cannot be described.

"I am a changed person in many ways. I know now I have control over my emotional state and have proven that to myself in the most dramatic fashion possible. The empowering feeling this knowledge provides cannot be described. I can't thank you guys enough."

Craig Bellgrove — Director, Fruit Property

Will have beneficial long-term effects

"Without doubt Mick Hawes has significantly contributed to the palpable increase in energy, enjoyment and output of my team. Too often team building/motivational/personal effectiveness type sessions have a limited life and are only 'feel good'. Whereas Mick's coaching seems to have provided a paradigm shift that will have beneficial longterm effects on each of us, and the team."

Bill Taylor — Employment Services Co-ordinator, Jobnet Tasmania

The feedback is beyond my expectations

"I have had first hand experience of the programs and have certainly found them to be of great value in both my personal and professional life. Many different departments have gotten involved with The Head Coach programs and the feedback is beyond my expectations."

Peter Gibson — Financial controller, Davies Bros Ltd

I found the tools and the focus to set and achieve goals

"I seemed to be flat out going nowhere, I had no goals... nothing to aim for. At the end of yet another torrid day, I grabbed the phone book and called Mick Hawes. Joining the program kick-started my motivation, I started to feel I had control over my life again. I found the tools and the focus to set and achieve goals. I deserve the rewards that have come with achieving my goals."

Tom Maggs — Australian Antarctic Division

TABLE OF CONTENTS

INTRODUCTION

"It is in your moments of decision that your destiny is shaped"
— *Tony Robbins*

This is one of my favourite quotes. The reason is, it can be put to use moment by moment in every area of our lives. In fact right now as you are reading this introduction you have the opportunity to make a commitment to yourself to read everything in this book and decide to put one new idea into practice every week, and do what you can to master just one idea. In 12 months from now you will have 52 awesome habits that will change your life forever.

Of course you can also choose to be a slave to your excuses. "I don't have time", "I'm too busy" or whatever you can come up with so you don't need to challenge your comfort zone, so you can slide into the massive sea of mediocrity with the masses.

In your hands you have information and ideas that have been generated from almost 20 years of research and experience in the area of personal performance and personal change. You have the opportunity to benefit massively without the significant time, effort and money that I have invested over that period, but you must act! That is the price you must pay for the benefits you can enjoy with this information. SO — GO FOR IT!

Mick Hawes

CHAPTER 1

HOW TO CHANGE THINGS THE EASY WAY

Firstly, I'd like to say that I really appreciate the opportunity you have given me to be your coach. In this book I will be sharing with you tips and techniques to help you move from stress to success. And I hope that you are one of the few people that will go ahead and take action, and use these ideas. I hope you are not one of the many that may just read the book and do nothing with it. But I know, because you're reading this right now, that you are one of the few who act, as opposed to others who just talk and wish for things to be easier.

To get the best out of this book you really need to be open-minded, like the old saying, "The mind is like a parachute, it only works when it's open."

Before I get started as your coach one of the most important things you need to be aware of is "Social Hypnosis", we get hypnotised by the beliefs of all the people that we surround ourselves with. To gain an understanding of some things from a different perspective you really need to put those beliefs aside whilst you are reading this book. You will be able to weigh up the ideas I am sharing with you and you can then decide what you want to do with them.

Together, you and I are going to go through a model for change: it is not the model for change it is 'a' model for change. There are many ideas out there but this is one that I have used for over a decade and it's made a significant difference to me and to the many thousands of others I have shared this with. If the way you try to change things in your life isn't working as well as you'd like, then give this one a shot.

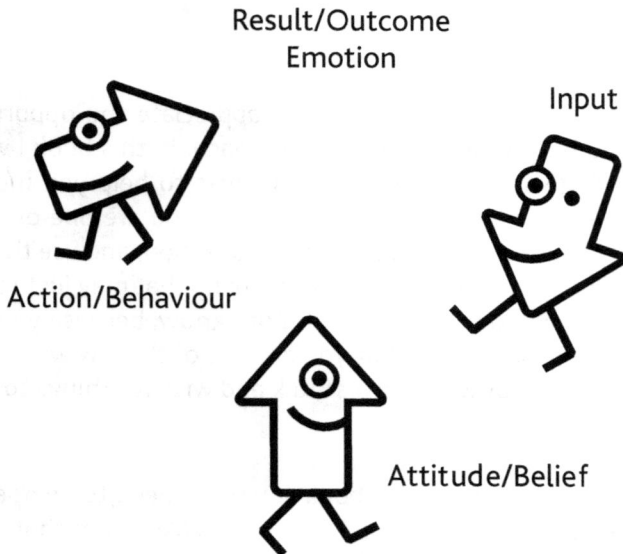

Result/Outcome
Emotion

Input

Action/Behaviour

Attitude/Belief

The first question I have for you is, do you experience emotions that you would prefer to experience less often? What would those emotions be called? Anger, frustration or fear? For the purpose of this exercise, I'm suggesting that the emotion is the end result. Your emotions or how you feel has a huge influence over how things turn out or the results you get. If you use this model you then have the opportunity to change the emotion. By changing the emotion you will get different results. Let's quickly walk through this model. This model says that if you want your results to improve, then how you feel needs to change. For example, if you are a sales person and you are always pessimistic and down in the dumps you are not going to sell a whole lot. Enthusiasm is the ticket for making sales and if you follow this model you will have an abundance of it. Or perhaps there have been times in your life when being calm would have created a great outcome in a certain situation but at the time "calm" wasn't even on the radar! If you use this model you will have a lot more control over your emotional experience.

This model says that how you behave, or in other words, how you move your body (body language) determines how you feel. If you don't believe me stop what you are doing right now, leap up and put the biggest, craziest smile you have ever done on your face. Now I bet you feel different doing this than you felt just reading the previous sentence. You may feel silly or embarrassed right now (that is, of course, if you actually did it and didn't just sit there like most people would) or perhaps you feel like laughing, but you do feel different. The way you use your body changes your emotions and in this model that body movement or body language is labeled as "behaviour".

CHAPTER 2

HOW TO CHANGE YOUR BEHAVIOUR

Now it's time to deal with actions versus behaviour. Social Hypnosis will have most people believing that your emotions are determined by what happens to you. However, I'm saying that the emotion is the end result of what you focus on with your thoughts and how you use your body language. So what needs to be altered to change your outcome? What has a direct impact on changing your outcomes and results? Think simply here, the answer is behaviour and action.

You may have heard of a guy called Zig Ziglar, I've been listening to him for many years. I once got the opportunity to see him live and I was amazed. He was over 70 years old at the time and was whipping around the stage like someone half his age. He talks about many very profound things and in fact, in his live presentations, he has to warn his audience when he is about to say something profound. He has found that if he doesn't warn the audience that he is about to say something profound, quite often they don't actually realise that he has said something profound. Zig says things like "if you keep on doing what you've been doing, you are going to keep on getting what you've been getting." Isn't that a mind-blowing idea? Do you think that's profound? Not many people think that idea is even slightly profound. If you don't think it's profound, you need to.

I coach many people and most of them desperately want things to change in all areas of their lives, and yet they do, say and think exactly the same thing, day after week after month, expecting things to be different! What sort of emotions do you think you would experience if this were the case? Frustration? Disappointment? So if you want to change what you get, you've got to change what you do.

What is the difference between action and behaviour? Right now think of someone you don't like very much. If you were walking along the street, feeling fairly good and you see that person walking towards you, what could you do, look the other way so as not to make eye contact? Or slip into a shop? There are many possibilities, but I guarantee with most people their body language would change. Their facial expression and posture would change in some way. This change may be mild, but there would be a shift. The other thing I can guarantee is that people don't think about which emotion would be the best one to experience in that situation, they just feel the automatic emotion that they normally feel under those circumstances. So what is the difference between action and behaviour? Action is something you consciously think of doing and then go ahead and do it, where as behaviour is automatic. The thought process behind a behaviour is a subconscious thought process. You only experience the behaviour, you aren't aware of the thought process behind it. Behaviour is a habit of action — an automatic action.

If you can identify times and situations in your life where your automatic action does not serve you well and re-engineer your automatic actions so that when you experience those situations in the future you will respond in a much more positive way, automatically! Would that be valuable to you? That's what I'm on about here. This isn't about positive thinking. The challenge with positive thinking is that you need to think about it. And if you leave positive thinking until you are challenged, you're not going to be able to do it.

Your input determines your output

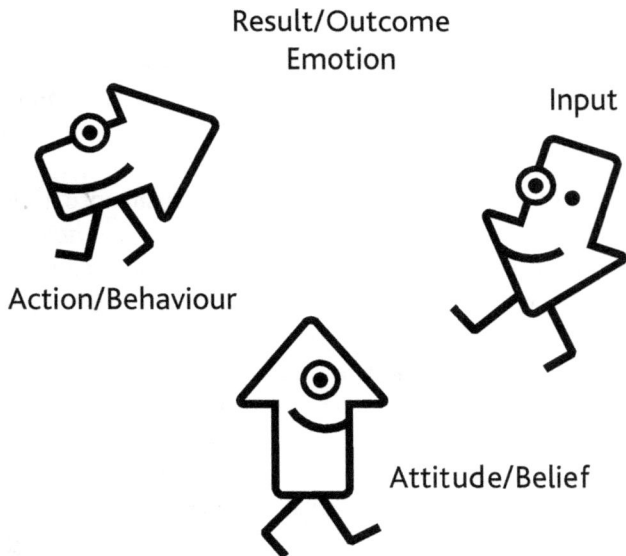

Result/Outcome
Emotion

Input

Action/Behaviour

Attitude/Belief

CHAPTER 3

HOW TO CHANGE THE BAD ATTITUDE

In this chapter I want to share with you my ideas for changing some negative behaviours into some more positive ones. Everyone has negative behaviours but only a small number of people are willing to change them, and I am betting you are one of those willing people because you are taking the time to read this book. So what drives action? What precedes action? And most importantly, what precedes behaviour? Preceding every action is a thought, a conscious thought, one that we are aware of. What I'm on about here is "attitude". What is an attitude? To me attitude is simply, a habit of thought. How do you create a habit? If you do something over and over and over, it becomes a habit. By repeating a thought process over and over, it becomes a habit, a habit of thought, an attitude.

Can you drive a motorcar? Cast your mind back to the very first time you got into a motorcar to learn to drive it. Can you remember that? How did you go? Your mental focus at that time, your conscious thoughts, were wrapped around the mechanics of the machine, thinking about the clutch, the brakes, the accelerator, the steering, the gears and that sort of stuff. You did a bit of practice and bit of repetition and eventually you started to get the car moving smoothly. Then you got your drivers licence.

Let me ask you a question, have you ever been late? You rush to the car, slap on the seat belt, scream out of the driveway and up the street. While you are doing this what are you thinking about? I'll bet none of your conscious thoughts were focused on driving. You would have been more likely thinking of an excuse to give your boss as to why you are late, again! When I ask people what they think about when they drive. Many people answer "nothing" or "just about everything except driving." Have you ever experienced ending up somewhere that you didn't mean to go? You're thinking about other things, listening to the radio or thinking about work, and when you snap out of your trance you realise you're in the wrong place. When you're driving now you don't think about the mechanics anymore.

Here's my next question, where did the thought process go that absolutely had to be there that first time you jumped into the motorcar to learn to drive? It's gone from a conscious thought process to a subconscious thought process. It is now an automatic thought process. It's a habit of thought that is driving the actions required to drive the car. If you were to put someone in a car that had never ever seen a car before and they were hurtling down a hill and someone pulled out in front of them and stopped. What would they do? They do not have the automatic thought processes anywhere in their brain to hit the brakes or steer the car. But if you've had some repetition, some experience, you will at least slam on the brakes to avoid a crash.

So attitude can be formed by repetition and if you repeat a thought process over and over again, it becomes automatic and it then starts to drive the automatic action. I am sure you can think of a number of behaviours you may have that don't serve you well and that you would like to replace with a better, more positive response. Well, part of the process is to stand guard at the entrance of your mind and monitor and choose some better thoughts. Whenever you pick up a negative or pessimistic thought, change it straight away. "That's easy for you to say" I hear you grumbling, well, just like learning to hit a golf ball or driving a car, if you practice you will improve, but it won't happen by itself. You must take action and follow this simple practice and you will be amazed at how quickly your automatic responses or behaviours will begin to change for the better.

Special Bonus Offer

If you would like more information on the strategies, tools and techniques available to help you grow your business or you would just like to follow me on this journey:

Visit this page to access bonus content that will help you apply the concepts in the book:

http://bit.ly/1tQhLCA

CHAPTER 4

YOUR INPUT DETERMINES
YOUR OUTPUT

Input is anything that can go into your mind. What you read, listen to and the people you hang around have a great influence on you. The thoughts you have, the words you use and your body language are powerful forms of input. To help you understand where I'm coming from with this, let me tell you a story... I went to a seminar that was held in an internal training room, the room had no windows. Before he got there the workshop leader had set up the room with some big posters over the walls with really positive quotes and positive sayings. I was sitting there reading these things and getting really excited. As I was looking around I noticed that in amongst these big positive posters there were a small number of negative posters, and they were only little — postcard size. I started thinking, "This is all a bit weird, what's this all about?" The workshop leader began the program and started to talk about how your input determines your output. The thing that makes the most difference to how your life turns out is what you allow into your mind. He said, "What I want you do to is imagine that this room is your subconscious mind, and all day long through the door, the entrance to your subconscious mind, this input comes in — your experiences, what you see, hear, taste, smell and feel. It's all being recorded in this amazing subconscious mind." Then he held up a torch and said, "I want you to imagine that this torch represents your conscious mind, and you are put in a position where you need to come up with a response, which is happening in almost every moment." So he was suggesting that your torch (conscious mind) is looking into your subconscious mind for these responses. He then switched off the lights. He moved the torch around the room with it switched off and would stop moving at random and turn the torch on. It would be shining on a poster and we would all read it. Then he turned it off, moved it around and at random shone the torch on another poster. He did this over and over until he finally turned the lights back on and asked, "How often did I land on a positive poster (a positive response) versus a negative postcard (a negative response) with my torch?" And what do you think the answer was? More often it landed on the positive posters. Why? Because there are more of them and they are bigger! Well, right there and then I had a "B.F.O.", a "Blinding Flash of the Obvious". It's as simple as that. It's all about what you allow in, which then determines what comes out. At the end of his presentation he suggested that we now start to stand guard at that the entrance to our mind and start to determine what comes in, because when we start to determine what goes in, we greatly influence what comes out.

So you see, your input really does determine your output. So go ahead and start to stand guard at the entrance to your mind.

CHAPTER 5

WORDS FOR CHANGE

There are a number of ways to stand guard at the entrance to your mind and the first one I want to introduce to you is the words you use. Our "Habitual Vocabulary" contains our most used words, these are our pet words and we use them a lot! The average person has around five to seven thousand words in their vocabulary. How many words out of this five to seven thousand words make up the Habitual Vocabulary? On average, about 170 to 250 words — not many! I want you to become a student of the Habitual Vocabulary. When you do, you will notice that most of the words are used to describe how you feel or how you're doing — outcome-type words.

When you become a student of the Habitual Vocabulary you will also notice that the negative words you use are really big, powerful words, such as "disaster", "horrific", or "traumatic". Words like these are used to describe day-to-day life experiences. When it comes to the positive words, well, they tend to have no power about them at all. Have you ever had a magnificent day? A day when everything went so well, it was just awesome? That day, when asked, "How are you going?" many people respond with "not bad" or "ok", or some other pathetic response. What you need to do is turn that upside down completely and start to give some power to the positive words and really take the power out of the negative words. I don't know how many times I have heard a conversation that goes like this:

"How was your morning?"
"Well, I just had a disastrous morning,
it's been absolutely traumatic."

When they are asked what happened that day for them to have such a dramatic response, they talk about things like, lost car keys, traffic hold ups and someone pinching their parking spot. You know, really earth shattering stuff! Not only do they use these powerfully negative words, but watch how they use their body language to give the words even more power.

Now, here's the reason why you need to be very careful with your choice of words. How many words does the average person speak in a minute? About 170 to 250 words per minute! If there are 170 to 250 words in your Habitual Vocabulary, and you speak at around 170 to 250 words per minute, you do the maths! Can you see any opportunity for repetition? That's what you need to be careful of. When you repeat something over and over, it becomes a habit! So if you change your words you can begin to change your habits. Just try it and prove me wrong. Start to become a "word detective" and listen to your words and other people's words and you'll be able to predict their future.

Before you read any further I want you to practice standing guard at the entrance to your mind and changing some of the words you are currently using. I want you to replace "frustrating" with "fascinating", replace "I have to" with "I choose to". Change "I don't have time" to " I chose not to do it". This is just a guide to get you started. I want you to do your best to replace any negative words or phrases that you currently use with positive ones and start to notice the difference it makes. In the next chapter I go a little deeper into the idea of watching your words, where you will see, if you change your words you can change your life!

Special Bonus Offer

If you would like more information on the strategies, tools and techniques available to help you grow your business or you would just like to follow me on this journey:

Visit this page to access bonus content that will help you apply the concepts in the book:

http://bit.ly/1tQhLCA

CHAPTER 6

CHANGE YOUR WORDS AND YOU CHANGE YOUR LIFE

Remember the words you consistently use in your day-to-day communication with others and your words will start to become your truth. The really neat thing about this is, if you do make a commitment to do something with the information I am giving you here, you will begin to enjoy the benefits of this incredibly powerful, yet simple idea very quickly. You see, words are just labels we use to give things meaning. Tony Robbins says, "Nothing has any meaning except for the meaning you give it."

Something happens and one person labels it as a problem and another person labels it as an opportunity. It is the same situation but you will find that each person will respond differently because of the label they chose. One of my favorite sayings is, "There are no problems, just opportunities brilliantly disguised." So I suggest that you begin right now to change your life and your experiences by choosing better words.

Instead of saying "problem" say
"opportunity"

Instead of saying "frustrated" say
"fascinated"

Instead of saying "I can't" say
"I won't"

Instead of saying "I have to" say
"I choose to"

Instead of saying "I don't have time" say
"I chose other priorities"

What are the standard "garden variety" responses to the question "Hi, how are you going?" "Fine", "good", "okay", "not bad under the circumstances". What we should be saying are words like "sensational", "unbelievable", "fabulous", "stupendous", and "absolutely spectacular and improving, thank you very much for asking!" (That last one is a quote from Zig Ziglar, a legend with this sort of thing). Would you feel like a genuine goose saying something like that? I do sometimes. The real key to this is repetition. Keep using these types of words and you'll notice a significant shift in how you feel for the most part.

How often during the course of a day do you get asked "Hi, how are you going?" on the phone or face-to-face? I know you get asked this question many times, perhaps hundreds of times, per day. Is that an opportunity to practice or what? Repetition, repetition, repetition — that is the secret here and many very educated and intelligent people just don't get it. Too many people don't realise how destructive the constant inflow of negative and disempowering words into their sub-conscious is. Change your words and you'll change your life!

Play with your words, have fun with them, but be sure to stand guard at the entrance to your mind and only allow the good stuff in. Always remember, your input determines your output. Words are probably the most powerful input, because changing your words has an impact on your conscious thought. Changing your words has an impact on your body language. After something that would normally frustrate you say, "I'm fascinated" instead of "I'm frustrated", and I guarantee that you can't maintain the frustrated body language. So your body language is going to change, which means your emotions are going to change — just because you changed one word. So now, really start to listen to your words and select words that will serve you well in the future.

Special Bonus Offer

If you would like more information on the strategies, tools and techniques available to help you grow your business or you would just like to follow me on this journey:

Visit this page to access bonus content that will help you apply the concepts in the book:

http://bit.ly/1tQhLCA

CHAPTER 7

THE LAW OF INERTIA

In the next four chapters I am going to cover what I call the "Natural Laws". I call them Natural Laws because I personally believe all of these laws work in the same way that gravity works. In other words, you don't have to concentrate on them or know about them, just like gravity, it works on you anyway. The first Natural Law I want to share with you is the "Law of Inertia". Do you know what inertia is? The dictionary defines inertia as, "The property by which matter continues in it's existing state of rest or motion in a straight line, unless that state is changed by an external force." Or in other words, "A body in motion tends to stay in motion, and a body at rest tends to stay at rest."

Now let me ask you a question. How much throttle does it take to get a plane in the air? Generally speaking, full throttle. So the pilot gives the engine full throttle and the plane goes up in the air and gets to a certain height and speed and then the pilot pulls the throttle back to cruising speed. Could the pilot get the plane to take off with the throttle set to cruising speed? Probably not. I use this analogy to help people to understand that when people try to change something in their life, like diet, exercise, saving money or getting organised they often violate this Law of Inertia. They either don't give the full throttle commitment needed in the beginning or they pull back the throttle too early, way before the change has become habitual. Anything you practice you will get very good at, so I would like you to begin practicing actions that will serve you well in the future rather than continuing to practice actions that will cause you pain in the future.

I want you to give this a go: pick something that you can do every day. (that is, seven days a week not just some days). Make it so damn easy that it's impossible for you to let yourself down. Be sure to choose an action that is not dependant on the weather, other people or on specialised equipment. In other words, make sure you can do it every day, no excuses! Sometimes when I ask someone what they have picked they might answer, "I will read a personal development book for 30 minutes a day" then when I then ask them how much they read now they answer, "none". As a rule, I don't like to put limits on people's goals and my experience tells me that very few people will succeed in making that kind of change. My suggestion is to make a commitment to read a minimum of just one line a day. You could do that easily. In your most freaked out, stressed out, out of control day you can still make that commitment. But most days you won't read a line, you'll read a paragraph, or a page, or a chapter.

The secret to succeeding with this idea is doing at least the minimum each day so you are learning to follow through with the commitments you make to yourself, instead of re-inforcing the habit of letting yourself down. Understand that you reinforce that bad habit of letting yourself down every time you don't follow through with a discipline you want to establish. It doesn't have to be reading, you could commit to a minimum of one sit up a day, or eat an apple a day, or smile at the third person you see every day. It doesn't have to be something that will give you a return, something big, the key here is doing something every day. This will establish a habit that will give you a great deal of confidence and self-esteem. And guess what? It can also be fun.

You will get the most from this idea on the days when you are really busy, under the pump, or just don't feel like it, and you still do your thing despite the challenges. The whole idea with the Law of Inertia is this: You go to workshops, or you get great ideas from reading a book, or listening to a recording and you get out there and you don't want to leave any of it behind. You want to do it all. It's the equivalent of running in seven different directions at once. Have you ever tried that? How far do you get? Not very far! How much energy do you use? Lots! Not the best plan. I'm suggesting that you identify one thing and absolutely commit to it. If you do the other things, then that's all well and good, but if you don't, it doesn't matter. Don't beat yourself up about it. But commit to this one discipline and focus on it. In a very short amount of time, you will notice the benefits of this crazy idea and you will be able to expand on it and commit to much more challenging things.

CHAPTER 8

THE LAW OF RECIPROCITY

The "Law of Reciprocity" is the second of the Natural Laws. The idea behind this law is, what you give out in life, you get back many times over. Many years ago I went to a live presentation by a man called W. Mitchell. He shared his life story with the audience. His story starts with him riding a motorcycle along the freeway, something distracted him and he turned to check out what it was. As his vision returned to the road ahead there was a truck in front of him and it was too late for him to do anything else other than to slide the bike along the road. The cap came off the petrol tank and the sparks ignited the fuel. There was an explosion and he turned into a human fireball. He suffered major burns to 65 percent of his body. In fact, the fire was so intense it literally burned his fingers off! He went on to talk about his recovery time in hospital and the great support he got from very positive friends and family members. Mitchell told how he got out of hospital and got on with his life. He created a large business, employing over 1,000 people. He ran for mayor of his town and would walk around with a big lapel badge on, saying, "Vote for me and I won't just be another pretty face."

W. Mitchell is just an amazing guy. He learnt to fly a light aircraft and one day he was flying and the plane crashed. In the crash he lost the use of his legs. So first he has the motorcycle accident, in which he suffers serious burns and loses his fingers, then he has the aircraft accident and is now a paraplegic, getting around in a wheelchair. Now I don't know that I would of thought of this, but soon after the aircraft accident, he figured that as he wasn't using his toes anymore, he may as well have his toes surgically removed and implanted up where his fingers used to be. He reckons that he is the luckiest man on the planet!

Now if he is the luckiest man on the planet, would you like to swap places with him? This man is an inspirational human being. He thinks he is very lucky because he gets the opportunity to travel around the world sharing his story, helping people and changing people's lives. The thing that I recall on a daily basis was the title of his speech, and it's all about the Law of Reciprocity. It's simply this: "It's not what happens to you, it's what you do about it." This law is about taking responsibility of where you are in life. Instead of pointing the finger out there at everybody and everything else, and blaming all of these external things for why your life isn't turning out the way you want, this law is about asking yourself what do I need to learn, or change, or overcome to live the life I want?

Years ago I heard a saying that is so relevant to this idea, "When you point the finger, have a look and see how many

30

fingers are pointing back at you." Do this for me right now, point your finger out in front of you and count how many fingers on that hand are pointing right back at you. Don't get me wrong, I am not talking about blame here, I am talking about responsibility, or as Dr Stephen Covey explains in his book, "The Seven Habits Of Highly Effective People", it's about changing the meaning of the word responsibility to "response ability" or working on your "ability to respond". Things happen in life and often these things aren't fair, but they happen anyway, and the best thing we can do is focus on how we respond. The more you work on having positive responses to life's challenges, the better you will get at it. But be aware, the more often you give away responsibility the better you will become at that. That is when life begins to drive you into a small corner and you feel as if you have no control over anything. So go back to some earlier chapters and revisit how to change your words, questions and body language and go to work on your response ability.

Special Bonus Offer

If you would like more information on the strategies, tools and techniques available to help you grow your business or you would just like to follow me on this journey:

Visit this page to access bonus content that will help you apply the concepts in the book:

http://bit.ly/1tQhLCA

CHAPTER 9

YOU ARE EITHER GREEN AND GROWING, OR RIPE AND ROTTING

The third law, the "Law of Never Ending Improvement" is all about the title of this chapter. "You are either green and growing, or ripe and rotting." Let's just imagine for a moment that there is a choice. Which one would you choose? The funny thing is that when I ask people that question everybody wants to choose "green and growing", but when you listen to their language, for the most part they are in the "ripe" mode and starting to smell.

Many years ago I was watching a program on television called "The Brain". The presenter was David Suzuki. This program explained how the brain works in a very simple way. It was a fascinating program. It began with pictures taken through a very powerful microscope, showing images of the brain making new connections with these things called Dendrites. When the vision was sped up it almost looked like the scene from the movie "Jumanji", when the vines are growing through the house. It explained that when we are learning something new, like a new skill, or even a new way of understanding something, the brain makes these extra connections with the growth of dendrites. So the more you learn, the more connections you have and the more connections you have, the more you can learn.

The program referred to a study of the brain in people that had diseases like Alzheimers and Dementia, and it was found that there was a group of people within the study group that had the disease but showed very little, to no signs of having the disease. They also noticed a group within a group of people that had suffered brain damage through physical injury who had made a much more rapid recovery to normal functionality. What did the two groups that either suffered less or recovered more quickly have in common? They were "green and growing". These were the kind of people who are always challenging themselves, they're always hitting the books, learning new things, going to seminars or being adventurous. They were very open-minded types of people. They were open to looking at things from a different perspective. The researchers concluded that the brain was so effective at learning, that the damaged portion of the brain's functions were taken over by other parts of the brain. The brain was able to learn how to do it very quickly. The same with the physical brain damage cases, their recovery was very rapid because the functions that were previously looked after by the damaged part of the brain were taken over by the undamaged parts of the brain. As I was watching this I thought, that's a good reason to challenge yourself and step outside your comfort zone as often as you can. It's like taking out some insurance for the future.

Imagine what's happening in your brain right now. There's stuff going on all over the place. As you challenge yourself to ask better questions, use better words, and re-train yourself to use better body language, the growth in your brain is going berserk.

The other part of the Law of Never Ending Improvement is "ripe and rotting"; you either use it or lose it. When you make the choice not to challenge yourself and stay in your comfort zone you also choose the consequences of that decision. My experience is that life is much more fun, exciting, rewarding and interesting when you are challenging yourself to be "green and growing", look for ways to do it daily. Read more personal development books like this one, listen to more recordings, and attend more seminars and workshops. And the best idea I have for you is, teach these ideas to who ever will listen.

Special Bonus Offer

If you would like more information on the strategies, tools and techniques available to help you grow your business or you would just like to follow me on this journey:

Visit this page to access bonus content that will help you apply the concepts in the book:

http://bit.ly/1tQhLCA

CHAPTER 10

THE LAW OF THE FARM

The "Law of the Farm" is the fourth of the Natural Laws. What do you think it might be? Well, it's a philosophy, a very powerful and valuable philosophy. If you have ever read Dr Stephen Covey's "The Seven Habits of Highly Effective People", you'll be familiar with this law. If you aren't familiar with this law and have read the book I suggest you read it again. In fact I think that you should read it anyway, as it is one of the best books on the planet and I would recommend it to anyone. In his book, Stephen says the best way to understand the philosophy of the Law Of The Farm is to understand it's opposite. The opposite philosophy is what he calls "Cramming Mentally". Have you ever sat a test or exam? Do you know what cramming is? Cramming is when you have plenty of time to study but it is left to the last minute and you pull an all-nighter and try to cram as much as possible into your head before the exam starts. Have you ever done a bit of cramming? I find when I ask people how they did using cramming, did they pass or fail, the majority say they passed. When I then ask how they felt when they found out they passed, they answer, "I felt relieved" or something similar.

The point is they felt a positive emotion when they passed using cramming. This can set up an "anchor" or "neuro-association" or in other words, a link between the cramming and the positive feeling in your nervous system. So you begin to feel that cramming is a good thing, even though you know that cramming is not the right way to learn things for long-term retention. Intellectually you know that but your nervous system doesn't. People then begin to take this cramming mentality into other areas of their life. That is part of the reason why so many people will buy a machine from an advertisement on television that "Will give you a full body workout in just four minutes a day" and then use it a couple of times and shove it under the bed to gather dust with the rest of the devices they have bought over the years. Or they try fad diet pills, drinks or supplements to lose weight but never really commit to mastering the fundamental disciplines of diet and exercise.

Now let's talk about the Law of the Farm. How successful would someone be if they went out and bought a farm and used their cramming mentality to run this farm? They might do things like this: a long weekend comes up, so they go on a holiday for three days and try to milk the cows a half a dozen times when they get back! How crazy does that sound? But it's not that much more crazy than some of the things I see people trying. The power of the Law of the Farm is doing the "seemingly insignificant things" every day. These are little things, like using positive and empowering words, asking high quality questions, and using more positive body language. If you do those every day, you will be blown away with the value that it can give you.

Let's play a game. I started to do this working in a jail many years ago. It was lots of fun. I want to give you two scenarios and I want you to choose one of them. I want you to choose one based on the effort required and the benefits you think you will get. The first option is, I want you to travel across town in the traffic to come and see me and we will talk for five minutes. I want you to do this every day for 31 days in a row, including Saturdays and Sundays. When you show up the first day I will give you one cent. When you return on day two I want you to give the one cent back and I will give you two cents. On the third day give me the two cents back and I'll give you four cents. We will follow this pattern for the full 31 days and on the 31st day you can keep the money I give you that day. The second option is, I want you to phone me one time, give me your banking details and I will deposit $25,000 into your account and it's all yours to do with what you like. I want you to think of your commitments, your work, the time, the travel, the cost, the whole deal. I want you to think of this as if it were a real offer. Okay, which scenario did you choose? When this is done in a live workshop, we would normally get about 50 percent taking each option. Many people who chose option one, the 31 day option, don't know why, they just chose it because they were suspicious. If you chose option one, did you know how much you would get on the last day? You would end up with $10,737,418.24, which is just a little more than $25,000. Now forget about the money because what I want you to take away from this is the principle of the Law of the Farm. By practicing positive actions and using positive words, thoughts and questions and repeating them over and over every day you will get an extraordinary result down the track.

Law of the Farm
(it's the seemingly insignificant that makes the big difference)

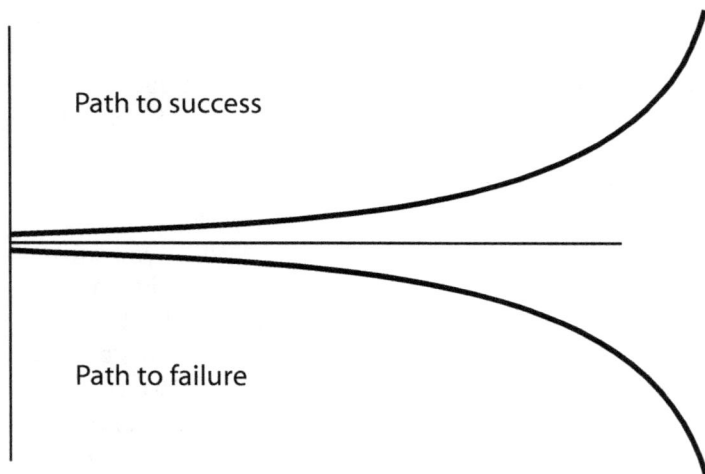

Path to success

Path to failure

I hope you are not too disappointed that I am only using this as an example and not really offering you option one. If you knew that you were going to get $10,737,418.24 at the end of the 31 days, you would follow through and turn up every day. I've said that if you change your words, your body language, your thoughts and questions you will change your life. But I have no way at all to prove to you that what I am saying really works. I know it works because of my experience. The only way you will know is through your experience, but you must give it a fair go. So I challenge you to apply the Law of the Farm for 31 days. Stand guard at the entrance to your mind and choose great words, great questions and use awesome body language every day for 31 days then you will see, feel and know the results for yourself.

CHAPTER 11

THE DREAM CATCHER

I am so proud of you right now! You are still reading, learning and growing when many others go back to old habits and just let life happen, but that's not you. So as a reward for your commitment, I have something very special for you in this chapter. It is easy, quick and fun, and it can have the most profound positive effect on you in no time at all. I call it the "Dream Catcher". What is the purpose of this Dream Catcher? Well, in essence it is simply an exercise to stretch the imagination. It will take 60 maybe 120 seconds a day. The beginning of the day is a good time to do this exercise. Start to write down the answers to the following questions: What would I like to have, achieve, experience, become, if there were no limits to time, talent or money? Now the key to this is to make sure that you write down things that you currently believe are impossible. To start with you may find this a challenge but most things worthwhile are a challenge.

In most cases people will write down things that actually are within their grasp, they could have or achieve but it will be hard work. That's not what I'm after. I want you to challenge yourself to not judge before you write, just write down what comes into your mind.

Often I get feedback from people saying they feel stupid writing things down that they could never have or achieve. This is something you will get past with persistence. You just need to understand that this is a stretching exercise for your mind, it is not a goal-setting exercise. The amazing thing with this tool is that when you follow the instructions and give yourself the opportunity to dream without limits, in a short time you will notice that in real life your thinking begins to change. You will have more confidence, greater self-belief and a bigger imagination, and you will find that you begin to come up with out-of-the-box ways to overcome life's challenges.

Right now I want you to go and find a piece of paper and a pencil. Do it immediately, don't put it off till later, let's do this right now! Are you ready? Ok, look at your watch and for the next two minutes I want you to write like crazy, do not stop, just let yourself dream! GO! Now I am assuming that you've done it. Start to have a look at what you've written down. Was it challenging writing some of those things down? I bet it was. Let's look at some of the things you wrote. How possible are they? If you think they are totally impossible for you in your lifetime that's exactly what I'm after here.

If you commit to this process every day, even if it's just for a minute you will get better and better and begin to think bigger and bigger. You will get comfortable with this way of thinking and it will start to affect your thinking in your day-to-day life. My experience with the Dream Catcher tool has been nothing short of unbelievable. When I look back at my early Dream Catchers the most amazing thing is that many of the things that I thought were impossible back then, have actually happened. I have found that the Dream Catcher opens your mind up to the abundance of opportunity that is everywhere and also prepares you to say "yes" to these opportunities. I now have the chance to travel around the world coaching and helping people, which was just a dream a few short years ago. Often I need to pinch myself to be sure that this is really happening.

If you commit to capturing your dreams without judgment you too will have opportunity come knocking on your door and you will be ready to open that door and say "yes"!

Special Bonus Offer

If you would like more information on the strategies, tools and techniques available to help you grow your business or you would just like to follow me on this journey:

Visit this page to access bonus content that will help you apply the concepts in the book:

http://bit.ly/1tQhLCA

CHAPTER 12

PRACTICE MAKES PERFECT

This chapter focuses on a subject that has only recently been brought to my attention: understanding that "practice makes perfect". Although I have been teaching this subject a fair bit over recent years I have just learned many new applications for it, so I've brought it forward a few chapters. I would have included it a little later in this book but I think it is so important that I should share it with you earlier rather than later.

There is a time to look at results and a time to focus on the process or the action steps required to get the result. I noticed the importance of this a number of years ago when I began doing work with some of the best junior tennis players in our country. I travelled around the country observing and coaching these very talented individuals. I always asked them this question, "What is the most important part of your game at this high level of competition?" "The physical part (meaning the skill and fitness), or the mental and emotional part?" In every case the answer was the mental and emotional part of the game, this was mostly because at the highest level of competition all of the players have a great deal of skill and fitness.

The second question I asked them was "How much time per day do you put into practicing the mental and emotional side of the game?" What do you think the answer was? You guessed it, "none". I couldn't believe what I was hearing. And this answer was consistent all over the country. The most important part of their game was receiving no time or attention. And even worse, when I observed the players practicing I would notice that every time they made a mistake, they would get frustrated and angry.

So let me ask you a question, what happens when you repeat an action over and over? That's right, it becomes a habit. So in essence, what these tennis players were practicing was anger and frustration, so guess what happened to them under the pressure of competition? They would get angry and frustrated when things didn't go their way, causing tension and tightness in their body. This didn't allow the athletes to play at their best, which in turn caused more negative emotions and the cycle just kept compounding until the players smashed their racquet on the ground or threw it over the fence!

Right about now you might be asking what has this got to do with me? How can this help me? Well, I think the same thing happens with many people. They practice negative emotions every day. There are many situations during the day when little challenges present themselves, and with a little bit of positive thought and discipline you could come up with a positive response, but you don't. You get a tiny bit angry or frustrated, take the easy way out and let your emotions control you. Most of us have a lazy approach to our emotional mastery.

Do you remember the "Law of the Farm"? One cent doubled every day for 31 days works out to be almost 11 million dollars. Well, you need to apply this law to your emotional life. See seemingly insignificant challenges as tremendous opportunities to practice your positive emotions. If you do this at every available opportunity, you will notice yourself having more and more positive responses to life's little challenges. You will amaze yourself at how different your emotional responses can be, even under the most trying circumstances.

So continue to ask yourself the question "What emotions am I practicing?" Practice does make perfect, but what do you want to make perfect? Your negative emotions? I think not. So make sure you are practicing the good stuff.

Special Bonus Offer

If you would like more information on the strategies, tools and techniques available to help you grow your business or you would just like to follow me on this journey:

Visit this page to access bonus content that will help you apply the concepts in the book:

http://bit.ly/1tQhLCA

CHAPTER 13

PREVENTION IS BETTER THAN THE CURE

Prevention is better than the cure. I'm speaking about this because I recently returned from the United States, where I had a fantastic opportunity to learn from the creator of the most amazing technique I have ever known for overcoming all sorts of fear, phobias, negative emotions, stress, anxiety, addictive behaviours and much, much more. Before attending a four day workshop we were asked to prepare ourselves by identifying ten challenging emotional issues that we would like to work on over the course of the workshop. I identified ten issues; they weren't huge but they were certainly significant and worth while working on. Throughout the workshop the leader would get somebody up on stage and work with them one-on-one. We, in the audience, were asked to follow along using the technique just as they were doing on the stage out front. The end result was that after the person on stage had finished their session (with spectacular results, I might add) around 80 to 90 percent of the audience reported a significant reduction or complete resolution of their own issue that they had identified before the session. In my case, after the first session, all ten of my issues became less intense. So for the rest of the four days I was able to observe and learn as much as possible. It was truly amazing and it was an incredible experience. The one thing that captured my attention throughout this workshop, and in many others that I have attended on the topic of change, was that even though the attendees were outstanding and caring people, many of them had no concept of prevention. What I mean by that is, they wanted to learn these techniques to help others with their emotional challenges and really believed in the value and the positive power of these techniques but had never stopped to consider how to prevent many of these emotional challenges from being established in the first place. They would overcome their list of issues and like a flash pull out another list. The issues seemed to be endless. However, I found it very difficult to come up with anything to work on.

Now please don't think that I don't have challenges, I do. What I am saying here is that my response to my challenges seemed to be different to the responses of many other people I observed. Every little thing seemed to be viewed as a major issue and caused drama in their life. I used to do that too, but having made a commitment to take a preventative approach to life, by guarding the entrance to my mind, many things that would have been a huge drama in the past, now simply are not!

Don't get me wrong here, I am just as excited about the potential of these techniques as the next guy. So much so that very soon I will be introducing you to and helping you master these amazing techniques. But I am convinced that you must have a commitment to prevention before you go crazy with the cure. Otherwise you will be always reaching for the cure and running the risk of thinking it doesn't work. After you have received the anti-venom to cure your snake bite, I think it is a wise move to stop playing with the snakes. In other words, these "Cure Techniques" are fantastic and we must make a commitment to stand guard at the entrance to our mind to ensure, to the best of our ability, we only let the good stuff in.

Special Bonus Offer

If you would like more information on the strategies, tools and techniques available to help you grow your business or you would just like to follow me on this journey:

Visit this page to access bonus content that will help you apply the concepts in the book:

http://bit.ly/1tQhLCA

CHAPTER 14

EMOTIONAL FREEDOM TECHNIQUES (EFT)

I think this is one of the most exciting chapters I have put together, as this subject has had the most profound effect on me and on many other people I have helped.

Do you experience negative emotions that you wish you could overcome? Anger, frustration, fear, anxiety, and the list goes on. Do you have compulsive behaviours that you wish you didn't have? Do you have chronic pain, like migraines?

If you answered yes to any of those questions I would like to introduce you to a technique that could work for you where everything else you have tried has failed. It is called EFT, "Emotional Freedom Techniques".

My first introduction to EFT was many years ago now, when I had the opportunity to attend a workshop called "Rapid Change Methods". I went just because the title of the workshop was what I was into; rapid change. When I was first introduced to this technique I didn't know what to think. At first I thought it was one of those things that seemed too good to be true, but pretty soon I found out that this was to be taken seriously, very seriously!

I was one of a number of volunteers that stood up in front of the group as a guinea pig, and what I had chosen to try the technique on was a pain I had in my jaw. EFT back then was predominately used on reducing and eliminating negative emotions but it was also mentioned that it worked quite well with physical pain, which was something I had at the time so I thought I would just give it a go. This wasn't just pain I had that day, this pain had been with me every day for many years. It had been diagnosed as being caused by me grinding my teeth at night and no doctor I had seen about it was able to help.

So as a guinea pig, I began applying this technique: using my finger tips to "tap" on specific points called "Meridian Points" (these are the same points that Acupuncture Practitioners use to insert their needles), whilst focusing my attention on my complaint by using certain phrases. Now if you think this sounds strange as I am explaining it to you right now, imagine how I felt standing in front of a group of people tapping on my head, face and upper body and saying that "I deeply and completely accept myself". I was thinking I wonder when someone is going to walk up to me and say "you're on candid camera".

Tapping Points

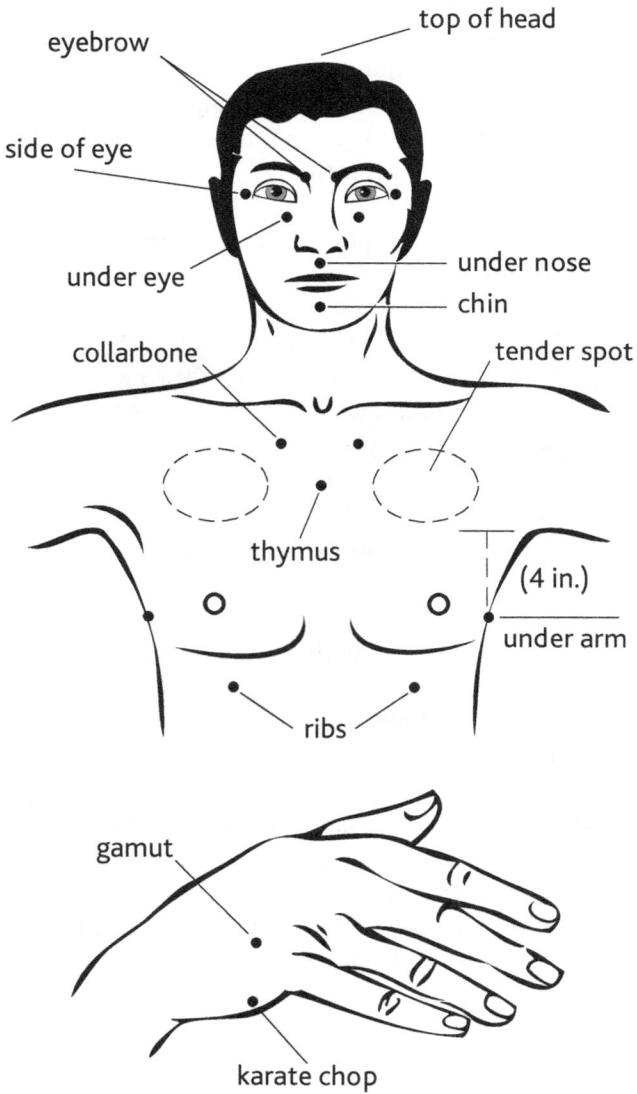

eyebrow

top of head

side of eye

under eye

under nose

chin

collarbone

tender spot

thymus

(4 in.)

under arm

ribs

gamut

karate chop

Well, that didn't happen, but what did happen was the pain in my jaw disappeared totally — a sensation I had not experienced in years. That got my attention and I immediately decided that this is well worth looking into and mastering. For the rest of the two days I was blown away by what I saw happen: from compulsive behaviours vanishing, to very deep seated phobias disappearing in just minutes. I was amazed, confused, excited but mostly, in awe of what I had seen and experienced.

Since then, EFT has become my preferred tool for change in almost every situation that I am asked to help with in my coaching business. The nice thing is, over the years I have discovered uses for EFT that can help people improve things that are already going well and not just fixing things that are broken.

One of the early profound experiences I had using EFT to help someone was with a lady who attended one of my live workshops where I taught some basic EFT. She called me a couple of weeks later and told me she had a water phobia that was so bad that she experienced terror every time she took a shower and she couldn't contemplate taking a bath. The thing was that she had been dreaming about joining the Police Force for as long as she could remember but couldn't even get a start, as the requirements to enter the Police training academy meant she had to be a proficient swimmer, but she couldn't even walk near a swimming pool, let alone get in.

I agreed to work with this lady. I did one half hour session away from water and two more half hour sessions at the pool. A couple of days later she phoned me and told me she was about to do her swimming test, and that when she was swimming she had to concentrate because she was now so relaxed in the water, she would sink!

In a car park a couple of years later I was approached by a Policewoman who introduced herself to me, it was the same lady. She had come to tell me she was now living the dream that she thought would never be possible. I was incredibly pleased for her. This is just one of the amazing stories I have been a part of since learning EFT.

This technique is simple to apply, easy to learn, and such a relatively painless way of overcoming the most deep-seated emotional issues. Obviously there will be challenges in your life where you may need the help of a trained EFT practitioner, but in many instances you can get great results being self-taught and applying the technique to yourself. When many people are starting out with EFT they don't just go ahead and do the tapping because they aren't sure whether on not they are doing it correctly. In my experience the worst that can happen is nothing. In other words, you have nothing to lose, so just get to it!

In the 8 years that I have been tapping I have discovered that one of the best times to tap is right in the moment — when you are feeling sad, frustrated, angry or scared. That moment is the right time because you are really tuned into the issue, so you can work on it straight away rather than relying on your memory or your imagination. The big challenge here is thinking to do the tapping while you are experiencing the negative emotion. For example, if you are feeling frightened, tapping may be the last thing you are thinking about. But I think in most cases it is possible, it just takes a little bit of thought and discipline.

EFT is an effective way to give up smoking. Tap whenever you feel like a smoke and commit to keep tapping until the desire subsides (in most cases, only a minute or two) and use phrases like, "I can do without this smoke and I deeply and completely accept myself", you will find it works brilliantly. The desire to have a smoke will gradually get less powerful and further apart. Unfortunately many people just go ahead and have a smoke instead of tapping and then come up with all sorts of excuses. Even if you just commit to tapping for one minute every time you want a smoke and at the end of the minute you still feel like having a puff, go right ahead, I believe a positive effect will still come about after a little while.

EFT is used for a mild headache, in many cases after doing some tapping the pain will actually change a little or even move to a different part of the head. You need to continue with the tapping and begin to do what is called "chasing the pain". Wherever the pain goes your focus must follow. If you do this you will find some, if not complete, relief. (Please understand that I am not suggesting this is a replacement for expert medical advice).

When you get a grasp on EFT, it will take you to another level of effectiveness. When you are working on an emotional challenge try to work out how that emotion shows up physically and tap on the physical side of the emotion, quite often you can get a good result in a short time. For example, if you have a fear of public speaking, imagine yourself being called upon to get up and address the masses, maybe you then start to feel the nerves kick in but specifically, how does your brand of nerves present itself? Do you get a tightness in the throat? Does your mouth get dry? Do you feel tightness or swirling in your tummy? How does your brand of nerves actually manifest itself? When you can identify these things begin to tap whilst focused on the physical issue. Work on all the physical issues and you may very well find that the fear has disappeared.

Also, when you are working on a physical problem such as a headache, migraine, allergy or a chronic pain somewhere in your body, work on the emotions that surround this physical issue. Ask yourself how this pain makes you feel. And then go to work on those emotions.

Special Bonus Offer

If you would like more information on the strategies, tools and techniques available to help you grow your business or you would just like to follow me on this journey:

Visit this page to access bonus content that will help you apply the concepts in the book:

http://bit.ly/1tQhLCA

CHAPTER 15

IT'S SIMPLE, GET ORGANISED

In this chapter I am going to begin to share with you some simple ideas about getting organised and self-management (many people use the term "time management" but you can't manage time, you can only manage yourself).

You might ask why I am talking to you about this subject, what does it have to do with stress? Well, let me ask you a question, have you ever had times when you felt out of control? And does this feeling of being out of control cause you to feel stress? I think the answer is quite clear; the two emotions can be inexplicitly linked. The solution is to learn some simple secrets of highly effective people.

My experience with this subject has been vast over the years and I have a genuine passion for it. The ideas that I am sharing with you have had a profound effect on my life and me. When

I first began my personal development journey I was working, on average, 14 hours a day, six and seven days a week. I am sure many of you reading this can relate to that. At the time I thought I could do things a little better but I wasn't prepared for the amazing change these ideas presented me with. Within three months of applying just a few basic principles I had cut my working day in half. Within 18 months I had changed things so radically that I was working around 14 hours a week. 14 hours a day to 14 hours a week! I was impressed.

I want to get you off to a flying start with your self-management, so I am going to let you in on the most powerful way to get results. It won't be how to use a diary, or set goals, or anything else that you would expect to find in a "Time Management" course, but it is how you think about the concept of time and how you communicate it to yourself.

In my experience, getting rid of phrases such as, "I don't get the time to do...", "I ran out of time" or "There just isn't enough time in the day" and replacing them with phrases such as, "I chose to do this" or "I am choosing not to do that" will change your decisions and behaviour. The bottom line is "I don't have time" is a flat out lie. You have 24 hours every day just the same as everyone else. What counts are the decisions and choices you make and the actions you take with your 24 hours.

By telling yourself that the actions you take are your choice, it puts you well and truly in control. When you tell yourself that time is to blame you are giving away control. Time cannot be controlled. Time marches on regardless of what you are doing. When you have the guts to tell yourself the truth, that everything in life is a choice, it will be one of the most liberating feelings you will experience.

CHAPTER 16

IF YOU DON'T KNOW WHERE YOU'RE GOING ANY ROAD WILL TAKE YOU THERE

Being clear about what it is you want is an idea that many people gloss right over. Where do you want to arrive? Who do you want to become?

In Stephen Covey's "The Seven Habits Of Highly Effective People" the third habit is "Put First Things First". This is his habit about time management. It requires you to make sure that you give priority to the most important things in your life. Stephen has also written a book called "First Things First". In this book there is a chapter entitled "The Main Thing Is To Keep The Main Thing The Main Thing". I don't think you even need to read the chapter to know what it's about. So to be able to keep the main thing the main thing, what do you need to know? That's right, you need to know what the main thing is.

I find it amazing how few people ever stop to examine what the main thing or things are for themselves. Many people don't find out until it is too late and they have lost what is important to them. The key issue here is the quality of questions you ask yourself. What I am on about here is, if you walked down the street and stopped 100 people and asked them "What do you want out of life?" 99 of them would give you a list of what they don't want. "I don't want to work in this dead-end job", "I don't want the debts that I have", "I don't want to be so stressed." So many people focus so much on what they don't want, and there is very little, if any, room in their thinking for what they do want. The challenge with this negative focus is that in many cases it becomes the self-fulfilling prophecy. In other words, what you think about most, you get.

I want you to begin to create a "compelling future" for yourself. I want you to create a vision for yourself that creates excitement, gets you up early and keeps you up late. I want you to commit to this process and I promise you that if you make this commitment, many of the things that cause stress, anger, frustration and the like will disappear. In most cases people feel those negative emotions just because there is nothing in their life to get fired up about. If you are waiting for something to come along for you to get fired up about, you will be in for a very long wait. You must make it happen!

Go ahead and do this. In the next chapter I will begin to share with you how to get started chasing your goals down.

CHAPTER 17

BALANCE: THE CORNERSTONE OF EFFECTIVENESS

If you followed the ideas from chapter 16 you have done some thinking and searching about the most important things in your life. Many people find doing that quite challenging and at the same time, very rewarding and exciting. As I have already mentioned, knowing what the main things are, is essential to gain control over your life, and reduce and eliminate the unnecessary distress. (Most people call it stress, but I like the distinction between good and bad stress. Good stress is when you challenge yourself to exceed your current boundaries and comfort zone, but you are in control. Bad stress or distress is when you have that feeling of being out of control). So it is also essential to have goals and objectives that challenge you to ensure you keep those main things as priorities.

What I want to suggest to you now is that you put some effort into creating goals that will also make certain that you have a focus on balance. This is done by having at least one goal in each of the following areas of your life.

These areas can be show in a circle:

Obtaining Balance

Personal Development

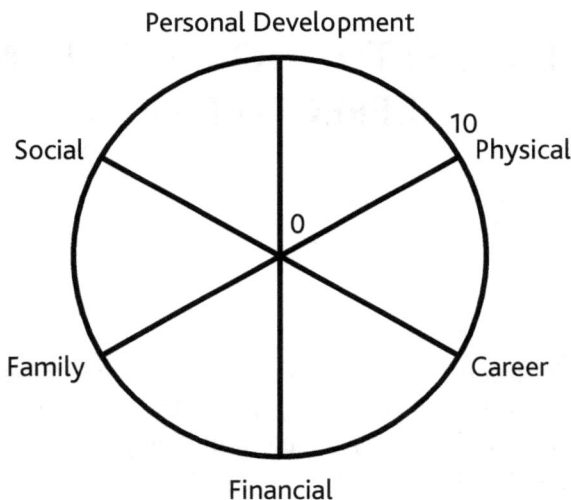

Having an objective in each area of life ensures that your balance will be a constant work in progress.

Balance is vital, as every area affects every other area. If you are not taking care of your physical area and you lack energy or you are ill, it will have an adverse effect on all of those other areas. Just as having financial trouble would also affect all of these other areas. I am sure you have experienced this or perhaps you know someone who has had financial challenges and it has had an impact on their family life, their health or their career performance. You see, everything affects everything, so I urge you to take the opportunity to begin to create a goal for each of the 6 areas (above) and go to work on them. The rewards will be more than worth the effort.

If you are having difficulty coming up with some worthwhile goals, it is more than likely your goal setting muscles need to be woken up because they haven't been used in a while. In many adults those muscles haven't been used since childhood. It seems funny to me that the more educated we get the less we use our imagination. The best thing I know to wake up those unused imagination muscles is the Dream Catcher, I covered that back in chapter 11, take a look at it again.

Here are some tips when writing down a goal. Follow the three P's:

1: Write it so it is Positive. For example, instead of saying I want to lose 5 kilograms, say I want to become and maintain 80 kilograms. In other words, tell yourself what you want, not what you don't want.

2: Make sure it is Personal. You need to know what the benefit is to you. And the goal needs to be "do-able" by you, so you don't need to rely on anyone else for the achievement of the goal.

3: Be sure that the goal causes you to have a Personality trait change. Who you become in the pursuit of your goal is far more valuable than the achievement itself.

CHAPTER 18

YOU'VE GOT TO MINE
THE DIRT TO GET TO THE GOLD

This chapter is short and to the point and it goes to the heart of pretty much everything in life, well, at least to the areas you want to improve.

I am sure you have now got your mind around the idea of setting goals for balance. However, it is interesting that often when I encourage people to set goals, to create a compelling future for themselves and to become clear about the steps needed to make it happen, the feedback is, "I'm just no good at setting goals." People sit down for five minutes and don't get inspired and give up. They have been so caught up in being busy and focusing on what's not going right in their life, that their imagination muscles are almost dead. If that is what is happening to you, you need to bring these muscles back to life with the Dream Catcher and with consistent goal setting. That's right — consistent goal setting, even if you think you're no good at it.

I once heard Zig Ziglar say, "If something is worth doing, it's worth doing poorly, until you do it well." And this seems to be the challenge for many people; they don't persist when they come up against some difficulty. You must set goals poorly before you find the goals that will get you up early and keep you up late. You must be willing to "mine the dirt to get to the gold." I know it will be worth it for you. Anything worthwhile in life is challenging and that is why we are drowning in a sea of mediocrity, because too few people are willing to do what it takes. But I know that is not you, because you are still reading these pages. I also know you need encouragement to follow through with my ideas.

So get moving, start to write the goals that don't inspire you and then throw them out and do it again and again, because every time you rise to that challenge you are getting closer and closer to the gold. Get started, keep going, get angry if you have to, but do it, do it, do it.

WHEN WOULD NOW BE A GOOD TIME TO GET STARTED?

Special Bonus Offer

If you would like more information on the strategies, tools and techniques available to help you grow your business or you would just like to follow me on this journey:

Visit this page to access bonus content that will help you apply the concepts in the book:

http://bit.ly/1tQhLCA

CHAPTER 19

MOVE THE GOAL POSTS

How often have you heard someone complain about "the goal posts being moved?" About how unfair it is? Well, I am going to suggest to you that moving the goal posts is not only good, it is invaluable and you must do it for yourself.

One of the reasons for doing this is, that the closer you get to the achievement of your goal the less "magnetism" it has. I am generalising here, as this is not the case for all people and all goals. I am sure an athlete competing in the final of the Olympic Games has just as much, if not more enthusiasm toward the achievement of this goal than they had when they began their training regime. I am talking about the people that haven't been great goal setters and are beginning this process.

In the people I have coached I have noticed that because they grow and improve, become more confident and have greater belief in themselves, the initial goal they created doesn't hold as much excitement as it did when they first set it. This is due to the personal growth that has taken place.

I suggest you look at your goals individually and ask yourself this question "On a scale of one to ten, ten being maximum, how enthusiastic and passionate are you about this goal right now?" If your answer is less than ten then ask yourself this "What would have to happen or what would I need to add or change to make this goal a nine or ten?" In many cases the original goal can become a stepping-stone goal in the pursuit of something bigger.

The secret here is to consistently ask the above?? questions so you keep re-setting your goals, rather than waiting until they have been achieved. I have seen many people go back-wards very quickly, by not re-setting their goals. After the achievement of a goal, and the high that is experienced, it can be very challenging to re-group and start again. Many times I have seen people just stop setting goals and stop growing at this point because it is all too hard.

You see, the great value in goal setting is not in the achieve-ment of the goal, but who you become, what skills you learn and the knowledge you gain in the pursuit. That's why goals must be challenging, so they force you to grow. It is this con-stant growth that pays the big dividends in life.

Goal setting is just like starting an exercise program; it's tough at the start but gets a little easier as you go. But how hard is it to start again if you have stopped for some time? You think of all the effort that has been put in already and that the benefits have all disappeared. You also remember the pain you experienced at the beginning last time. All this adds up to making a new start less desirable. It's better to have kept it up in the first place.

Make goal re-setting a habit. I believe that by doing this your goals never become overwhelming. You will be creating success for yourself habitually! Wouldn't that be a better habit than some of the other habits you have right now? We are all slaves to habit, so start designing habits that will give you the life you really want, rather than a life full of negativity.

Special Bonus Offer

If you would like more information on the strategies, tools and techniques available to help you grow your business or you would just like to follow me on this journey:

Visit this page to access bonus content that will help you apply the concepts in the book:

http://bit.ly/1tQhLCA

CHAPTER 20

A VERY RARE SKILL INDEED

As I am writing this I have the headphones on and I'm getting down to "Play That Funky Music White Boy" by Wild Cherry — just to give you an idea of my age, generation and music tastes. The interesting thing that came into my head as I began to write while listening to music was the effect it has on my emotional experience.

Normally I write in complete silence and get into the emotions I write about, which are sometimes not the most positive emotions when I am trying to get people to take action through the written word. While listening to all my favourite tracks from the past, I find it very challenging to feel any emotions other than enthusiasm and a general feeling of fun and positivity.

This is just a simple observation from life as it happens, but it is yet another example of how your input determines your output. This also has nothing to do with the subject I had intended to share with you in this chapter, so I had better get to it.

The skill I am referring to in the title of this chapter is the skill of self- appreciation. I guess on reflection, my opening comments do have plenty to do with this subject, as what you focus on most tends to have a huge effect on how you feel, the decisions you make and the actions you take. In my experience coaching individuals and sports stars, and speaking to groups, many people tend to focus more on what they didn't do today, what they missed out on, what they haven't got and so on. I'm sure you get the idea. Even people who have amazing skills, people who work really hard, people who accomplish phenomenal things on a daily basis, still feel frustration, anger, distress and other negative feelings, along with a general lack of fulfillment.

Why is this the case? I am betting you might even know the answer to this having read this book so far. That's right, the input determines the output.

Some years ago a wonderful lady came to our company searching for help and answers. The lack of progress toward her goals was creating a lot of pain for her. Over the next year she did an incredible amount of work to change her thoughts, words and actions. In just over a year she had achieved things that neither her nor I would have thought possible in a very short period of time. Amazing!

Some time later I ran a workshop that this incredible lady attended and I asked the participants what they would like to personally work on. When it came around to this lady's turn she indicated she would like to get to work on her health and take it to a higher level. When she explained what she wanted to work on she referred to the accomplishments of the past year in what I thought was a very dismissive way. My response was not as calm as perhaps it should have been, I guess this was because I couldn't believe her lack of appreciation for her previous accomplishments. This led to me seizing the opportunity to do a whole impromptu workshop on self-appreciation.

There is a principle I talk about when teaching Time Management that states: "When you feel good, you do well and when you do well, you feel good." This creates an upward positive spiral. Also, "When you feel bad, you don't perform so well, and when you perform poorly, you don't feel so great." This process creates a downward negative spiral. Which one would you prefer? The thing is, I think we have more control over our emotions than our results. That being the case, the secret is to focus your attention on your accomplishments, what you did do rather than what you didn't. Focus on your strengths rather than your deficiencies.

In Australia, we have a sport called Australian Rules Football. One of the most successful players and coaches in that sport is Leigh Matthews. In my corporate coaching I use a lot of Leigh's Team Building philosophies. One of the things he often says is "In an effort to make a person perfect we hone in on their imperfections, thereby sapping their confidence." We do this to ourselves. We constantly remind ourselves of our weaknesses, deficiencies and imperfections. And in the process we drive our self-esteem and confidence spiraling downward. Leigh also promotes the philosophy of "If you've got a problem, fix it, if you can't fix it, ignore it." That's a very simple approach and I think it's an effective one, but it is a philosophy that most people will not subscribe too. I encourage you to subscribe to it. It works!

I suggest you also subscribe to an idea I discovered from the incredible Tony Robbins: the idea of morning power questions. Create a list of just a few questions you can ask yourself every morning. What can I be proud of in my life today? What opportunities can I enjoy today? Who do I love and who loves me? I'm sure you can make up some more for yourself. Don't worry too much about finding the answers, just commit to asking the questions daily and the answers will come in their own time.

Special Bonus Offer

If you would like more information on the strategies, tools and techniques available to help you grow your business or you would just like to follow me on this journey:

Visit this page to access bonus content that will help you apply the concepts in the book:

http://bit.ly/1tQhLCA

CHAPTER 21

TEACH WHAT WE MOST NEED TO LEARN

"Teach what we most need to learn." I heard Tony Robbins say this many years ago and I think it is a very powerful statement. I also heard Dr. Phil say, (Yes, that's right I watch Dr. Phil every so often) "We tend to see our deficiencies in others." So the focus of this chapter is about using your own example to influence others, and the side benefit of this is that you enjoy the benefits of your own good habits and disciplines.

I am often asked, "How can I get this other person to change?" When I do seminars or workshops and the subject matter is poor habits and behaviour and how to change them, it is amazing how easily peoples' thoughts drift away from themselves and onto others. I guess this happens because it's easy.

It's easy to identify the faults in other people and it's hard to make changes in our own life. It is hard because our focus is more often on the "sins of others" rather than on our own challenges.

This also tends to happen when a person begins to make some progress with his or her own personal development and begins to learn how destructive negative input can be. They begin to judge others rather than putting their energy into their own development. In many cases when one person in a relationship begins to grow faster than the other, personal development itself can become a wedge between them.

Earlier I mentioned a quote from Australian Football coaching legend Leigh Matthews, "In an effort to make someone perfect we hone in on their imperfections." The best tool you have to influence others is your own example. If your energy is put into your own skills of listening, emotional management, time management and everything else we have covered together over the last 40 pages or so, you will enjoy the benefits of your new disciplines and your example can become a very powerful thing to help others change.

Now having said that, let me warn you that the way you use your example is the real key here. I suggest you become the "quiet achiever". Don't push your new-found knowledge and skills onto others or keep throwing the benefits you have experienced into the faces of others. I have experienced this myself and seen many others go through this "evangelistic" phase. I have learned some life-changing idea and of course, everyone else must know! I know that in the past I have pushed people away with my enthusiasm, so I have learned to be a bit more laid back with my approach and only give my advice when it is asked for. This is quite challenging sometimes because you want to help, but at the end of the day, advice not asked for tends to be very ineffective.

So what has the title of this chapter got to do with this then? When you do have people who ask you questions, or want your advice or input it is a very valuable opportunity for both parties. They get some great information, and you benefit in two ways. The first is, if you are to teach, you must learn thoroughly. Secondly, you have just put yourself "out there" which means there is an expectation from others that you hold yourself to a higher standard.

So become the "quiet achiever" and use your energy to work on your own disciplines, skills and thoughts. Do this and you will find others will follow your excellent example.

Special Bonus Offer

If you would like more information on the strategies, tools and techniques available to help you grow your business or you would just like to follow me on this journey:

Visit this page to access bonus content that will help you apply the concepts in the book:

http://bit.ly/1tQhLCA

CHAPTER 22

PROCESS VERSUS RESULTS

I would like to share an idea with you that really became powerfully clear to me when I started work in the area of elite sports: knowing the difference between the result and the process to get the result, as well as knowing the appropriate time and place to focus on each area.

Have you ever played sport or just a game and got angry or frustrated? I bet you have, I know I have. I have found that when I have analysed the cause of the anger or frustration, in most cases the anger and frustration was due to a focus on the result. In sport, in most cases, the result is not always up to you.

Let me give you an example. When you are playing tennis, you can hit a series of great shots but your opponent hits a shot past you that is just plain too good for you to get back, or they accidentally hit the top of the net and the ball dribbles over the net and you lose that point. Is it helpful for you to get angry or frustrated with that? Not really. As you have read in previous chapters your emotional experience and your body language are inexplicably linked and the body language of anger and frustration generally has significant muscle tension involved. To hit the ball with power and accuracy, to move quickly across the court requires you to have smooth, flowing movements, which are almost impossible to achieve with your body full of tension.

The secret here is to have a focus on what you can control such as your self- talk, your breathing and body language, moving your feet in a quick fashion and so on. This puts you in the best frame of mind and you have the best body language you can have, which will give you the best chance of performing to the best of your ability. Notice I didn't say you would win, I said it would give you the best chance to perform at your best, and if that is good enough to win, great, if not, you did all you could, you gave your best.

Is this easy? No, it's not easy, particularly if you practice focusing on the results and not the process. Remember, whatever you practice you will become great at. So if you practice focusing on the result and getting frustrated and angry when things don't go your way, you will become a master at anger and frustration. But if you practice working on your processes and give yourself encouragement and great self-feedback for working on those processes, you will succeed more often than you would if you always focus on results.

When do you focus on the results then? You decide what it is you want, the goal, the result. Then work out the steps needed to get there (the process) after that, whenever you are thinking about your goal just work on the process. You can stand back and check your progress against your goal regularly, but not while you are working on the process.

If you find that this process isn't working as well as it should you can go ahead and change or refine it. If you judge your process while you are doing it and get upset that it's not working the way you would like, at that point you aren't giving your process a fair go. So my suggestion is to identify your goals, work out the process to get there, work on the process, and from time to time check your progress and adjust your process if needed.

Using this approach I have helped tennis players improve their rankings, cricket players set records, and golfers shave many strokes off their game. With this idea I have helped business owners and corporations transform their businesses. If you use this idea there no telling what you could accomplish.

CHAPTER 23

THE INTERPRETER

Are you an interpreter? The answer is yes. The question should really be, are you a positive interpreter?

I can hear you scream, "What are you on about?" Well, it's all about this incredible power we all have. A power that so many people use to create pressure, frustration, anger, stress and just about any other negative emotion you can think of. The power I'm talking about is the power of interpretation.

In Stephen Covey's book "The Seven Habits Of Highly Effective People", he says something I find incredibly profound, "The way we see the problem, is the problem." In other words, how we choose to see a situation has an effect on us and on our emotional response, as well as the potential value we may get out of the situation. For example, over the years I have lent people books and on occasion it has been the abovementioned book, (which, I might add, in my opinion is the best personal development book ever written) or it may have been a recording by Zig Ziglar. When the book or recording has been returned I would often ask how they liked it. Some people would rave about the content while others would give me very negative feedback.

Some people would complain about Zig Ziglar's American accent. On one occasion after returning "The Seven Habits", someone said to me, "What Mr Covey fails to realise is, I have to deal with idiots." This person had completely missed the message in the book. The people that complained about Zig's accent also totally missed the incredible messages he was offering, simply because their interpretation was "this is a load of American hype." In both cases, it really was a situation where the way they saw the problem was the problem. Had they interpreted the information in a different way there is no telling what amazing and life changing ideas they would have learned.

You have the opportunity to interpret your situations moment by moment, and you have heard me say often in the past, "Whatever you practice you get good at." So if you practice interpreting your situations in a way that causes you to see them as problems, you will become a master at spotting problems. And soon enough problems will be all you will see. If you practice interpreting your situations as opportunities, you become a master opportunity spotter, and you guessed it, after a while all you will see is opportunities.

So let me ask you a question, would you rather be met with a day full of problems or opportunities when you get out of bed in the morning? Because it is up to you; you and no one else.

Many people reading this may be thinking that I live in a dream world, not in "the real world". Well, I live in the same world as everybody else, where there are taxes, traffic, inflation, pollution and crime. But I choose to do the best I can at any given moment and interpret my world in a way that allows me to feel good and see abundance and opportunity. And by the way, I don't have a mortgage on seeing things this way; you can do it too. It is simply a choice. A choice that gets easier the more often it is made.

If after reading this chapter you feel you didn't learn anything, or it didn't help you in any way, or you think you have heard this all before and it didn't do anything for you last time either, I suggest you go back to the beginning of this chapter and interpret it in another way, a way that gives you value!

Special Bonus Offer

If you would like more information on the strategies, tools and techniques available to help you grow your business or you would just like to follow me on this journey:

Visit this page to access bonus content that will help you apply the concepts in the book:

http://bit.ly/1tQhLCA

CHAPTER 24

SUCCESS IS INCONVENIENT

I heard a lady at a seminar say, "Success is built on your inconvenience, not your convenience." Having been involved with Personal Development and Performance Coaching for a long time now, I can say that this is one of the biggest stumbling blocks I witness.

People often come to me asking for help, and in most cases present their challenges as if they are destroying their lives. So I provide some suggestions as to what actions could be taken to overcome these issues and turn them around. The person takes off with renewed vigor and enthusiasm back to their life. When next we speak I am told, "I haven't had a chance to do those things I was supposed to do." Which basically means that the issues aren't important enough to do anything about!

I once had a lady ask me to help her overcome a "significant emotional issue" (her words), as she seemed upset about this issue. I offered her a time to meet the following day. She replied by saying that the time I offered would be inconvenient, as she was going to a party that afternoon and didn't want to look like she had been crying. I instantly suggested to her that perhaps the issue she had just spoken to me about is not really a big deal after all, and that she could call me some time in the future if she needed my help with a "real issue". She took off, disgusted at my lack of compassion.

I bumped into her some time later, at which time she told me the horrible things she thought about me after our last conversation, but then she came to realise that it was the jolt of reality she needed to start changing some things in her life. She then went on to tell me about some of the wonderful things she had done since we met and how she was enjoying things in her life now.

Many years ago when I was working in a sales position I had begun to perform well and often led the sales team in sales figures. I believe this was a result of the effort I put into myself and into my development through reading, listening and attending a lot of training seminars. Other sales people (who were often getting poor sales figures) would ask me to help them to improve their sales results. When I told them about the reading, listening and attending extra training they soon lost interest in my help. Why? Because it wasn't convenient. They wanted the success, but were not willing to put in the time and effort to get it.

Does a champion sports person train only when it's convenient? No. They know that it is critical to their success so they give it the priority is deserves.

Let me ask you a question. How many ideas have you read about in this book, which you think are great ideas, but you haven't gotten around to using?

If you want change, improvement, and success in any area of your life, you must give the activity needed to make it happen the right priority, and almost always it's inconvenient! That's great, that's exciting, that's awesome! Why? Because that makes the possibility of you succeeding much greater, simply because the majority of others won't do what you will, just because it is inconvenient for them to do so. That's why it is so crowded at the bottom of "The Ladder of Success". There is plenty of room further up the ladder, as only the people who are willing to do the "inconvenient activities" are up there. Are you willing to join them?

I remember a quote from Walt Disney that kind of sums this up, he said, "If you want to be successful, look around and see what the world is doing, and don't do it!" Identify what you want to change. Find some information to help you change, then give it the priority it deserves. We have a saying here at The Head Coach, "The difference between doing it and not doing it, is doing it!"

Special Bonus Offer

If you would like more information on the strategies, tools and techniques available to help you grow your business or you would just like to follow me on this journey:

Visit this page to access bonus content that will help you apply the concepts in the book:

http://bit.ly/1tQhLCA

CHAPTER 25

THE MOTHER LODE GOAL

I am frequently asked many questions about procrastination and not maintaining disciplines; going back to the "Same ol', same ol". I hope this idea will help answer those kinds of questions. It's called "The Mother Lode Goal".

Mark Victor Hansen taught me this idea. I'm sure it has been around for a long time; it was just that Mark was the person who brought it to my attention. If you haven't heard of Mark, he is the author of "Chicken Soup For The Soul" which I believe has well over 100 different versions.

I was listening to Mark speak at a conference in Los Angeles some time ago and he mentioned this idea of the Mother Lode Goal, and I had the privilege of having lunch with him afterwards where I was able to discuss this amazing idea in more detail.

So what is it? The Mother Lode Goal is a goal that is so big that just the thought of it fills you with enthusiasm and passion. It is a goal so huge that almost everyone you tell about it thinks you are crazy and need to be locked up. Is this something that anyone can just sit down in one afternoon and come up with? I very much doubt it. There are some things I think you need to have done a substantial amount of first, and that is, dream catching and goal setting. I have covered these ideas in previous chapters.

The thing with the Mother Lode Goal is that it has this magic ability to get you up early and keep you up late, in other words, it creates positive energy, as opposed to negative energy from stress and other damaging emotions, that just drain your energy at days end. It also helps you keep things in a positive perspective, so you don't get distracted and brought down by all the little niggling negatives. More importantly, it causes you to maintain focus and activity in all areas of life. You must have a balanced approach to life to be able to pull off something of this magnitude! If you need to refresh this concept in your mind flip back to the chapter that unpacked this idea of balance.

So here is the challenge for you. Start catching dreams, begin writing down your goals, even if they don't fire you up with enthusiasm and passion yet, be prepared to mine the dirt to get to the gold. Have a go at seeing if you can come up with your Mother Lode Goal, one that you even think you are crazy for thinking of.

CHAPTER 26

IF YOU WANT TO BE SPONTANEOUS, YOU HAD BETTER PLAN FOR IT

It seems that there are many people who are challenged by planning and using a diary effectively. Often I hear this comment, "All this planning and goal setting doesn't allow me to be spontaneous." I respond by quoting the title of this chapter, "If you want to be spontaneous, you had better plan for it." This may seem contradictory but it is "oh so true".

My first lesson with this concept was when our family moved back to the Australian state where I grew up and I started the "Day Timer" distributorship. I was working around 14 hours per week and had just bought a yacht, which was moored in the bay at the front of our home. I thought this was heaven.

Most days I was out sailing or fishing or sometimes just sitting and looking around. The thing I found the most challenging about the situation was finding someone to play with. I had many friends, as this was where I grew up, but many of them ran their own businesses and were their own boss, however, they could never seem to be able to just drop things and take advantage of a magnificent day when it presented itself. But I could. I had worked very hard over the previous few years to learn some fundamental self-management skills and one of them is "High Quality Planning". This method of planning is excellent from the perspective of being able to have control over your day and week, to the point that if a wonderful opportunity presents itself, at a moments notice, you can re-organise the plan and go and enjoy yourself. To me that is being spontaneous.

One function of a high quality plan is being like a set of scales, where you can measure the importance of one thing against another. If you get asked to do something, you can weigh the consequences of not doing it against the consequences of not doing the most important task on your plan. This causes you to always be doing the most important things. But it only works if you have a plan. Without a plan your scales have nothing on the other side to weigh other things against. This creates a habit of reacting instead of being in control and deciding what to do next based on consequences.

Another function of a high quality plan is knowing what needs to be done by when. You can see all the parts of your day, week or month in front of you, like the blueprints for a building, so you can see the effect of moving things around. This allows you the luxury of being spontaneous. My experience has taught me that without the plan, and it needs to be a high quality plan, spontaneity is rarely on the radar.

CHAPTER 27

IS YOUR PLAN
A HIGH QUALITY PLAN?

Here are the prerequisites for a high quality plan:

1. It must be written.

2. It must contain both work and personal tasks.

3. It must have a priority assigned to each task.

If your planning doesn't have all three of these prerequisites covered, it is not a high quality plan. So lets look at each of these parts separately.

Your plan must be written. This simply means that the time you are working things out while you are having a shower or driving to work is not long enough to create a high quality plan. It must be written down so, as I mentioned in the last chapter, you can see all of the parts to the plan like a blueprint for a construction. Getting all of the parts to your plan written down on paper also allows your brain to be working full-time on decision making and creating positive solutions to your daily challenges, rather than being clogged up remembering things like what to do next. Another benefit of a written plan is that it helps you plan logistically and geographically smarter. In other words, you can begin to group tasks together that can be done when you are in a specific location and cut down your travel time. But apart from all that, just having your day, week and month planned out on paper in front of you gives you a great feeling of being in control of your life, and that's got to be of benefit.

Your plan must contain both work and personal tasks. This is, of course, on your days at work. Balance is essential for effectiveness. So by creating the habit of always making sure that you have personal tasks to perform every workday, it keeps a focus on balance. Most people that actually plan, which aren't many, tend to plan in the workplace. This tends to mean that only work tasks make it onto the plan, which then leaves no room for personal life. It is easy to see why many people become workaholics and get stressed out. All they think about is work, all they plan is work. They get out of balance, and become stressed and ineffective. To be effective you must have balance, to have balance you must plan for it, not just hope for the best.

It never ceases to amaze me that so many people put effort into planning their workday and put no effort at all into planning their personal life, and which part of their life is really more important? Well to answer that question, ask yourself,

"What would I do if I only had a few weeks to live?" I seriously doubt you would say to yourself, "I've only got a few weeks, I'd better go to work!" Now I'm not saying that work isn't important, I am simply saying put things into perspective and begin to put at least some effort into planning your personal life.

Within your plan have a priority assigned to each task. There are many different priority systems but the one I have found the most valuable is a simple A, B, C, D system. It becomes really powerful once you have a clear understanding of what each letter really represents. I will unpack the meaning of this priority system in the following chapter.

Special Bonus Offer

If you would like more information on the strategies, tools and techniques available to help you grow your business or you would just like to follow me on this journey:

Visit this page to access bonus content that will help you apply the concepts in the book:

http://bit.ly/1tQhLCA

CHAPTER 28

CATEGORIES AND PRIORITIES

How have you been going with your High Quality Planning? When done properly this method will give you a tremendous sense of control over your day, week and month. It doesn't need to take forever to do, the secret is understanding how it works and just following the guidelines from the last chapter. The real kicker with this process is understanding and applying categories and then priorities. That is what you will discover in this chapter.

Once you have created your "List Of Things To Do Today", you then need to put each event into a category. Just before I launch into that let me again tell you that for this to be as effective as possible, the entries you put on your list really need to be action steps related to the goals you have set for yourself, so you are working on things that you have previously decided are important. In my experience, many people just make up their list (if they do a list at all) with things that they think they "have to do", but in reality these actions are not getting them any closer to the achievement of their goals. These things make the list, most often, because they have some sense of urgency about them, but urgency has very little to do with importance. I will share this whole idea of urgent versus importance with you in the next chapter. But for now, do your best to ensure that your list is made up of action steps from your goals.

Okay, so you have your list written down, you now need to decide what category each entry fits into. We are going to use the A, B, C, D system. For you to be able to do this effectively you will need to understand what each letter represents. "A" represents an activity that is "Vital". The dictionary defines the word vital as, "Essential for Life". "B" represents "Impor-tant" and there is a significant difference between vital and important. The easiest way to remember this is to relate A to "heart and lungs" and relate B to "arms and legs". If you lose an arm or a leg, your life will continue but it causes some is-sues that you will need to adapt to, whereas, if you lose your heart and lungs — it's all over.

I have found the easiest and best way to decide if something is an A or a B is to ask, "What will happen if I don't do it?" This helps you to make a decision based on consequences, rather than using your gut feeling, which is usually directed by a sense of urgency and not importance.

"C" represents something that has "some value" and "D" rep-resents "a complete waste of time". Hopefully you won't use D much, but keep an open mind and ask the question "What will happen if I don't do it?" If the answer is "nothing" then make it a D and don't do it.

Once you have given each entry in your list a category, you now give each of the A's a number so they are numbered most vital to least vital. So you will end up with A1, A2, A3 and so on. Then do the same with the B's and C's.

Now that you have completed the list the next challenge is to do each of the things on your list in the order that you set out. This is not as easy as you may think, particularly if you haven't done this before. Your natural tendency will be to just do things as they come up or as you think of them. If you have trouble saying "No", if you ever have a feeling like you haven't achieved what you wanted to that day, if you ever procrastinate, if you feel like a "crisis manager", then this is the answer for you. As with most things in life that are rewarding, this will be challenging, but I can promise you that if you use this in the way I am suggesting, this plan will have a profound effect on your productivity and on your stress levels.

Special Bonus Offer

If you would like more information on the strategies, tools and techniques available to help you grow your business or you would just like to follow me on this journey:

Visit this page to access bonus content that will help you apply the concepts in the book:

http://bit.ly/1tQhLCA

CHAPTER 29

THE IMPORTANT
VERSUS THE URGENT

Are there urgent things in your work and personal life? Do you feel the pressure to take care of all those urgent things? I know I did and I didn't like it. Many years ago I was very fortunate to have a wonderful man take me under his wing and encourage me to begin to fill my mind with life-changing ideas. His name is Ian. He lent me his copy of Dr Stephen covey's book "The Seven Habits Of Highly Effective People". This amazing book provides far too many benefits to mention. However, the one I want to share with you now is the "Time Management Matrix". Pictured below is a diagram of the Time Management Matrix.

The purpose of this diagram is to help explain the difference between an activity that is important, or urgent, or both and what we tend to do when we are presented with these activities.

	Urgent	Not Urgent
Important	**I** ACTIVITIES: Crises Pressing problems Deadline-driven projects	**II** ACTIVITIES: Prevention Relationship building Recreation New opportunities
Not Important	**III** ACTIVITIES: Interruptions Some phone calls Some mail Some meetings Popular activities	**IV** ACTIVITIES: Trivia Some mail Some phone calls Time wasters Pleasure activities

In the top left hand quadrant, quadrant 1(QI) you will see that this represents an event that is both important and urgent. You could call this a "crisis". What do people tend to do when presented with a crisis? They tend to act. The same tendency is also there with QIII events as well, but QIII events are only "urgent". When the question "What will happen if I don't do it?" is asked the answer is "not much". So a QIII event is not important, but we feel a sense of urgency, so we do it.

QIII events are those things that after you have done them you find out it was a waste of time. There are many of these events in our day, but because we are creatures of habit, often we just don't pick them up.

QII is the place to invest your time and energy. QII events are things that fall into the three categories of planning, preparation and prevention. If you put effort into planning, preparation and prevention, what effect will that have on your QI events? They will go down! You will have less crisis to deal with. If you have less crisis to attend to, doesn't that then mean you can invest more time into planning, preparation and prevention? And so the cycle goes.

How do you begin this process? Well, you need to identify some QIII activities so you can say no to them and use that energy to work in QII. In the next chapter I will pass on to you a special way to find these "time thieves". But before you move on to chapter 30 see if you can find some activities in your day that aren't important, yet you feel a compulsion to do them anyway. Say no to them and use that time to do some High Quality Planning as set out in the past few chapters.

Having been able to really understand that the urgent doesn't really have anything to do with importance has been one of the profound learnings for me over the years.

Special Bonus Offer

If you would like more information on the strategies, tools and techniques available to help you grow your business or you would just like to follow me on this journey:

Visit this page to access bonus content that will help you apply the concepts in the book:

http://bit.ly/1tQhLCA

CHAPTER 30

HOW TO CATCH A THIEF

How did you go creating a High Quality Plan? Were you able to find any QIII activities? Did you discover anything that you felt compelled to do, but when you asked the question "What will happen if I don't do it?" the answer was "not much"? I certainly hope so. Finding these types of activities can free you up both time-wise as well as emotionally.

Now I want to give you a very simple process to follow that will give you a clear understanding of where all of your time, energy and effort goes. If I were to ask you how much of your day is invested in the really high priority things, and how much of your day is taken up with distractions, interruptions and other low priority and no priority things, what would your guess be? Would it be 50/50, 70/30, 20/80? Well, at the end of the day it is just a guess and you are using your gut instinct to answer the question. Would you like to actually know where the time goes?

It is a very simple process, one that I believe was the turning point for me. When I did this exercise I was so disgusted by the result I vowed to myself to change the way I was living and I did. I think that if I had not done this exercise, the time management information that I had learned might well have just sat on the shelf and would never have been put into practice to the level it did. So what I am saying here is, this is essential. It is a little like navigation; to be able to plot a course to where you would like to end up, firstly you must know where you are.

I thought at first that my day would have broken down to around 20/80, that's 20 percent on the important stuff and around 80 percent of my day was spent with the distractions, interruptions and other low or no priority rubbish. After I did this exercise I found that the truth was closer to 5/95. How would you feel if you had just realised that you were wasting 95 percent of your life? Well, disgust isn't a powerful enough word to describe how I felt. But that realisation drove me to make the changes that have provided me with a great lifestyle. You too can have a lifestyle that you can enjoy, but first you must be willing to face the truth, and do the work!

So I want you to do a time log, write down (just in dot point form) the things that you do in your day from the time you get up until the time you go to bed. Do this in around fifteen minute chunks. Your most likely reaction to this will be, "You want me to do what?" Well, the reality of doing it is dramatically less overwhelming than thinking about doing it. The benefits of doing it will be overwhelmingly worth it.

Just write down what you have been doing all day. I want you to do this for a minimum of seven days in a row. The big secret with this process is honesty. The worst person to lie to is yourself, so don't doctor this up so you can feel okay with it, just capture the activities, don't judge them just capture them. We will work out what to do with this information later.

I am very confident that if you do this, and I say "if", because I can tell you that the majority of people won't do it, you will be blown away by the amount of time you can free up to really work on building your dream life. But to do that maybe you need to get really dissatisfied with your current life rather than just putting up with it. So I enthusiastically encourage you to do this and over the next few chapters I will share with you how to benefit from the information you gather with this exercise.

CHAPTER 31

SOMETIMES THE TRUTH HURTS

One of my favourite sayings is. "A little pain never hurt anyone." What I mean is that often, emotional pain gets us to move. Things like fear of loss and other negative emotional experiences get us to take action, often in attempt to avoid more pain in the future.

How did you go with your time log? There is a very great chance that many of you reading this right now could be feeling a slight tinge of guilt because you didn't do the time log! Well, life is all about choices, and if you choose not to do it (and I think you have read enough of this book to know that an excuse like "I don't have time to do it" won't wash with me), you also choose to not enjoy the benefits that this exercise can deliver. The great thing about choice is that you can make a new one every day. So if you didn't do it, I encourage you to make the choice to do it, starting today.

What did you learn from recording your activities? Often just the act of recording what you get up to every day can have a positive effect. The real benefit from doing the time log comes from firstly knowing what your goals are. For this to really deliver the goods you must have clarity about what your goals are for your professional life as well as for your personal, family and social life.

If you know what your goals are, you can simply question each event on your time log, "Is this part of the plan for achieving my goals?" If it is, you can give it a rating A, B or C. "A" being vital, "B" being important or "C" creating some value to the pursuit of my goals. If the activity is not related to your goals it is a "D" equating to a complete waste of time. Of course, you can rationalise that any activity can be part of your goals. And if you have read "The Seven Habits Of Highly Effective People" you will have learned the real meaning of the word "rationalise" by splitting the word into two words "rational-lies". As I have said before the worst person to lie to is yourself. So to get the best from this time log exercise you need to be honest with yourself. You need to take a "warts and all" look at your activity and choices, and if what you see is painful, then change it.

By applying the A, B, C, D to your time log and then using some simple maths you can work out what percentage of your day is invested in the A's and B's and what percentage of your day is spent in the C's and D's. If the reality creates pain for you I hope it is enough to get you moving on changing some things. Or maybe the time log shows you are already very effective and there are some areas that can be refined. Either way, you win.

In my experience, I have found that there are many people who use more time coming up with reasons and excuses as to why their lives aren't turning out the way they would like, rather than actually doing what it would take to live their dreams. Don't be one of those "excuse" people, take an honest look at your choices and actions and you will find activities that you can say "No" to. Don't do these things anymore. This will free up your time to work on the things that will make the big difference.

If you look at each of the entries on your time log and ask, "What would happen if I didn't do this?" often the answer will be "nothing." When I did this exercise for the first time, I found that a huge chunk of what I did, if I never did it again, would make very little difference in my life. So I stopped doing those things and started to use this time to read personal development books, attend seminars, set goals and do high quality planning, and within just a few short months I had found that I had cut my working day in half, as well as improving my productivity.

If getting those sorts of results interests you then go right ahead and get started. I was once asked "There are two kinds of people, excuses and results, which one are you"? What a great question!

Special Bonus Offer

If you would like more information on the strategies, tools and techniques available to help you grow your business or you would just like to follow me on this journey:

Visit this page to access bonus content that will help you apply the concepts in the book:

http://bit.ly/1tQhLCA

CHAPTER 32

PUT THE BIG ROCKS IN FIRST

Dr Stephen Covey, if you haven't already gathered, has been a big influence for me over my personal development journey. I remember listening to a live presentation where Dr Covey asked a volunteer to fill a big jar with some big rocks about the size of your fist. Dr Covey then asked the audience if they thought the jar was full. A few people said that it was full but many suggested that there were a lot of air gaps between the rocks, so the jar wasn't full.

Dr Covey then asked the volunteer to empty some gravel into the jar to fill all of the gaps between the big rocks. After this was done the audience was again asked if they thought the jar was full. This time more people thought it was full, but a few said that the gaps still existed, they were just smaller.

So the volunteer was asked to pour sand into the jar to fill all of the gaps. He did this and when the audience was asked the question about the jar being full almost everyone suggested it was full, apart from a couple of people who insisted that there was still some gaps between the grains of sand. So the volunteer was asked to pour water into the jar until it reached the top. After this everyone was happy that the jar was full.

Dr Covey then asked the audience what they could learn from this demonstration. Different people came up with many answers like, "There is always room to do a little more" and so on. The real value from this demonstration comes by answering this question "If you didn't put the big rocks in first, would they fit?" The answer is simply, no!

The secret with this is understanding what the big rocks represent. They don't represent the big jobs or big tasks, they represent the most important things to you in your life. What this demonstration is suggesting is that you ensure that the most important things in your life are planned in your schedule. Make sure that your plans, long-term and short-term, contain these things. If you choose not to put these things in your plan first, there is a huge chance that you will get caught up with distractions, interruptions and heaps of low leverage, urgent but not important things, leaving no room for the most important tasks, ideas and objectives in your life.

Try this exercise, right now, don't put it off because you are busy. Just do it! Write the numbers one to ten down the side of a piece of paper, and then quickly write down the ten most important things to you in your life. Don't even think about reading on until you have done it!

I reckon that most of you struggled to even write ten things down quickly. This is because many people never really give this much thought, they get on with their life and never really unpack this idea. So if you have done a list of the most important things to you in your life (and it doesn't matter if you have more or less than ten) I now challenge you to go back and look at the time log you should have done and see how much of your time is invested in maintaining and being involved with the things on your list. While you are at it, see how much time you spend on things that aren't on your list.

This exercise may give you an insight into becoming clear about the activities you choose and the decisions you make on a daily basis. Like I said some time ago. "If you don't know where you are going, any road will take you there." So be sure to put your "big rocks" in your daily, weekly and monthly plans first. Because if you don't, they won't fit!

CHAPTER 33

JACK OF ALL TRADES, MASTER OF NONE

"Jack of all trades, master of none," I am sure that you have heard this saying. I find it to be true in the personal development world. I have a tonne of ideas, techniques and information that I want to give you but I want to be sure that you don't become a "Jack of all trades".

The ideas I am passing on to you have the potential to transform your life, if put into practice and constantly refined. So I would like to take this opportunity to encourage you to take up a simple challenge. But first you need to answer this question. Are you willing to invest a little over 30 minutes over the next week on an activity that can create inspiration, motivation and endless positive outcomes for you in your life?

If so, read on. I'll keep this very short so you can just get to it.

STEP 1
Go back and skim through every chapter in this book.

STEP 2
Give yourself a mark out of ten as to how well you think you have done with each message.

STEP 3
Ask yourself this question, "In relation to each topic, how well am I putting it into practice?"

STEP 4
If the answer is, for example 5 out of 10, then write down some actions you can take to make it a 7, 8 or 9 out of 10.

STEP 5 — TAKE ACTION!

Special Bonus Offer

If you would like more information on the strategies, tools and techniques available to help you grow your business or you would just like to follow me on this journey:

Visit this page to access bonus content that will help you apply the concepts in the book:

http://bit.ly/1tQhLCA

CHAPTER 34

FUN COULD BE THE KEY

How did you go with the exercise from the last chapter? Did you find some things that you had let slip? More importantly, did you find things that you have mastered, so you can give yourself a great big pat on the back?

Here's an idea that I heard quite a few years ago listening to a Tony Robbins recording, he called it "A" class activities. Tony had this idea that the activities we do everyday can be divided into A, B, C and D class activities.

An "A" class activity feels good when you do it, it is good for you, it is good for others and it serves the greater good.

A "B" class activity, doesn't feel good, but it is good for you, it is good for others and it serves the greater good.

A "C" class activity, feels good when you do it, isn't good for you, isn't good for others and doesn't serve the greater good.

A "D" class activity, doesn't feel good, isn't good for you, isn't good for others and doesn't serve the greater good.

A Class Activities

Activity Class:	Feels good	Is good for you	Is good for others (team)	Good for Business
A	Yes	Yes	Yes	Yes
B	No	Yes	Yes	Yes
C	Yes	No	No	No
D	No	No	No	No

If you have a think about this idea, it makes sense that many people tend to do A and C class activities where the common denominator is "it feels good". If you really think about the things you do in your life, for many people, the C class activities outnumber the A class activities significantly.

The secret to enjoying the benefits from this idea is to ask yourself the question, "How do I turn my B class activities into A class activities?" For instance if you don't like running, but you know it does you good, brainstorm some ideas like, listening to your favourite music while you jog, jogging with someone you enjoy being with, or running in new and different places. In other words, add the "fun factor". The limits with this are in your imagination and we already know that the Dream Catcher can expand your imagination.

So what are you waiting for? List as many B class activities as you can and get busy turning them into A's. And finally, see if you can come up with some clever ways to take the fun out of the C class activities, so you will do them less or stop completely.

Special Bonus Offer

If you would like more information on the strategies, tools and techniques available to help you grow your business or you would just like to follow me on this journey:

Visit this page to access bonus content that will help you apply the concepts in the book:

http://bit.ly/1tQhLCA

CHAPTER 35

MORE ON INPUT

Way back in chapter 4 I unpacked the idea of input. Now I want to share with you an idea that was suggested to me many years ago, when I began getting interested in personal development. This idea ties into the "Your input determines your output" theory, as well as turning your class B activities into class A activities.

I learned that what you put into your mind on a regular basis has a huge impact on how things turn out in your life. At that time I tried to read but just couldn't get into it. I hated reading. I had read one book in 31 years and it was called "Invaders From Space". People who I was meeting through my personal development journey were always recommending books to read, but I just couldn't commit to reading on a regular basis. It was a genuine class B activity.

I was covering a lot of miles in the car every day so I was listening to lots of personal development recordings. In these recordings the people were always recommending books to read. I knew I should be reading them but I just didn't have the desire. Then one day, on a recording I was listening to, the speaker mentioned, if you read about a certain subject for just 30 minutes a day, within a couple of months you will be reasonably knowledgeable on the subject. If you continued your 30 minutes a day of reading, within a year you could be regarded as an "expert" on that subject. He continued on to say, which was the clincher for me, that if you continued to read on a specific subject for just 30 minutes a day, after 10 years you would be considered a world-leading authority on that subject.

Now, I didn't know if that was true, but is sounded good to me, and I had a dream to help as many people as possible benefit from the amazing information I was learning in the field of personal development. In that split second of hearing this idea, reading went from a class B activity to a class A activity. That little bit of information turned my perception of reading upside down.

That was well over 10 years ago, and I don't know that I am a world-leading authority, but this book will be read by people in over 40 different countries around the world. What I do know is the that this small shift in thinking opened up a whole world of knowledge, ideas and techniques that have transformed my life and the lives of many thousands of others that these ideas have touched. I certainly hope that somebody reading this book will have the same experience and fall in love with learning and sharing this incredible information. So hit the bookstore or the library or surf the net for some e-books and find something you can get passionate about.

CHAPTER 36

TAKE YOUR OWN TEMPERATURE

Now I want to introduce you to a simple theory regarding re-setting and testing the "magnetic pull" of your goals. Often the most exciting and motivational time with goal setting is at the beginning, when you are thinking about the achieve-ment of the goal and all the wonderful emotions you will ex-perience when you get there. For many people (other than the most diligent and disciplined), as you get into the activity needed to achieve the end result, your focus often changes from the wonderful feeling at the end, to how this looks and feels like just plain hard work. When this happens the mag-netic pull of the goal starts to weaken. If this goes unchecked there is a huge probability that progress towards the achieve-ment of the goal will slow to a halt and potentially start you along the track of thinking that goal setting is a waste of time and never give it a go again. You will start to believe that goal setting just doesn't work or you are just no good at it.

So I suggest that you look at a couple of preventative measures. The first is to look at the activities required to achieve your goal and ensure you have created some class A activities, not class B activities. The second is to ensure that the inspiration is high when thinking about the achievement of the goal. Sometimes this can be done by re-setting your goal so that the original goal becomes an action step for a much bigger goal. It is important that this is done well before the achievement of a goal as there is no motivation in an achieved goal, and there is a danger that the goal setting process will stop. If this happens, it is very difficult to get started again — the Law of Inertia comes into play: "A body at rest tends to stay at rest." We want to use the other part of this law: "A body in motion tends to stay in motion." Basically the message here is to be constantly taking your own temperature, or in other words, checking your level of motivation and excitement about your goals and if the reading is low be sure to do something about it straight away.

CHAPTER 37

EMOTIONAL FITNESS

Often when I do seminars and workshops I get asked questions like, "How do you stay positive all the time?" When I tell the person that I don't, I get angry and upset, they get a bit confused. I guess this comes about because they think the idea of getting into personal development is to "eliminate" negativity. My view is a little different. I think "Emotional Fitness" is the thing to work on. Let me explain.

I equate emotional fitness to physical fitness. One way to test your physical fitness is to measure how long it takes you to get back to your standing heart rate after vigorous exercise. I like to measure emotional fitness in a similar way. How long does it take you to get over some anger or negative emotions and get back to a feeling of control and lose that negativity? The faster you can do that, the more emotionally fit you are.

Like physical fitness, emotional fitness needs training and practice. I suggest that you go back and visit some of the previous chapters and get practicing and improve your emotional fitness.

Special Bonus Offer

If you would like more information on the strategies, tools and techniques available to help you grow your business or you would just like to follow me on this journey:

Visit this page to access bonus content that will help you apply the concepts in the book:

http://bit.ly/1tQhLCA

CHAPTER 38

BODY LANGUAGE

I am not going to talk about body language and how to read it, however, I want you to know that your body language is a powerful way to manage your emotions. I believe that the way you use your body has a huge impact on how you feel. If you do some experimenting you will find that it is impossible to look happy and feel sad, or look sad and feel happy.

If you start to experiment with facial expressions, how and where you breathe (for example, full and from the diaphragm or shallow and from the upper chest), how quickly or slowly you move your body, as well as gestures such as a clenched fist or completely relaxed limbs, you will notice how different you feel when you change how you are using your body.

Probably the most noticeable changes come from facial expressions. Just play around with this idea and soon you will be able to identify that when you do certain things with your facial expressions you feel a particular emotion. The ideal would be to find the facial expressions that create the emotions you like and then practice them. Do this and you will find that you will be experiencing these good emotions more often. In other words, practice your emotions. You can do this just about any where and any time. Above all, have fun with this. The rewards will be huge.

Special Bonus Offer

If you would like more information on the strategies, tools and techniques available to help you grow your business or you would just like to follow me on this journey:

Visit this page to access bonus content that will help you apply the concepts in the book:

http://bit.ly/1tQhLCA

CHAPTER 39

DON'T PLAY THE BLAME GAME

One of the things I have found that eliminates stress and increases a sense of control is taking personal responsibility. This means, "not playing the blame game."

I remember many years ago listening to Zig Ziglar for the first time. He said, "You are who you are and where you are because of what has gone into your mind." It may be a simplistic view but I think for the most part it is true. I also remember listening to a recording by Jim Rohn, where he told a story of a meeting he had with his employer and mentor early in his working days. He was asked why he hadn't reached any of the goals he thought he would have reached by this stage in his life. Jim's response was swift, as if rehearsed. He rolled out a list of reasons that contained things like inflation, the government, bad luck, people that wouldn't help him and so on. After Jim had finished giving his boss all the reasons why he hadn't succeeded in life in the way he had intended, his boss turned to Jim and said, "Mr. Rohn, that was an impressive list of reasons, but I noticed something wrong with it." Jim asked, "What?" and his boss replied, "You ain't on it."

It is easy to blame something else or give away responsibility. In fact it seems to be almost encouraged these days; if you trip over when you a walking down the street, by the time you have picked yourself up off the ground you have thought of half a dozen people to sue, instead of saying to yourself, "I really need to watch where I'm going."

Stephen Covey, the author of "The Seven Habits Of Highly Effective People" says, "If you want things to change, first you must change."

It seems to be a rare person who asks how they need to change or what they need to learn to overcome life's challenges. This is a skill and can be learned by the repetition of the right action. What is the right action? Well that depends on what you are trying to change or achieve, but I do know there is no end of information to help you with whatever you are trying to accomplish. The libraries are chock-a-block full of it (and a library card is free). The bottom line is: you need to take personal responsibility.

To follow up Jim and his mentor's conversation: Jim was asked how many books he had read, how many seminars he had attended and how much written goal setting he had done in the past year to help him achieve his goals. His answer was "None".

I suggest that if people used just a fraction of the energy, time and effort that they use on coming up with excuses and blaming, and put that energy into learning new skills and refining their philosophy, things would be considerably different.

CHAPTER 40

THE NEW YEARS RESOLUTION

You may be reading this at the beginning of a new year or not, it really doesn't matter. The "New Years Resolution" method of creating change or improvement in your life works just as poorly any time of the year. What I mean by this is, the big majority of new years resolutions last only days, hours, minutes or never even get off the ground. Some just last until you sober up. For most people, this use of a deadline for massive change just doesn't work long-term. You know the type of change I mean, when people say, "I'll give up smoking after I finish this packet" or "I'll will be getting on the exercise program starting Monday" or "I will start to eat healthier after the holidays."

Cast your mind back to chapter one, I introduced you to a model for change that basically states that if you want to change the result you must change your input. In the model for change the four parts are: Input, Attitude, Action/Behaviour and Result/Outcome.

Your input determines your output

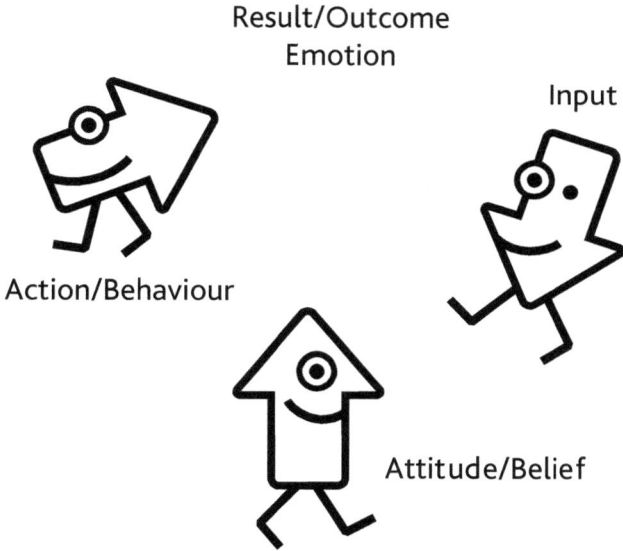

Result/Outcome
Emotion

Input

Action/Behaviour

Attitude/Belief

When you use a deadline to create massive change, as in the new years resolution, you are trying to change the behaviour and the result that behaviour is giving you, without changing the attitude, or in other words, the thought process driving that behaviour. Also, in the case of the new years resolution style of creating change, the input, or the information about the habit you are trying to change, does not change.

So basically, a new years resolution is trying to create a change in behaviour but leaving the old thought patterns and subconscious beliefs in place. No wonder it's tough! If you want to change your behaviour, have a look at the beliefs and attitudes that support it and then go to work on changing the input (words, thoughts and information) surrounding that behaviour.

Special Bonus Offer

If you would like more information on the strategies, tools and techniques available to help you grow your business or you would just like to follow me on this journey:

Visit this page to access bonus content that will help you apply the concepts in the book:

http://bit.ly/1tQhLCA

CHAPTER 41

FINANCIAL IQ

Often people make financial new years resolutions. I thought it would be worthwhile to cover some simple ideas about finance, as it is a subject that is associated with stress, it is often the trigger for arguments, and sometimes it is the cause of failed relationships.

What is "Financial IQ"? I think it is simply the way we think about finances, money, investment and so on. In chapter 39 I mentioned Jim Rohn and his conversations with his mentor. In one conversation Jim's mentor asked him, "Mr. Rohn, in the last six months, how many books have you read about financial management and how much money have you invested?" Jim answered "None". If you were asked that same question, what would be your answer?

If you haven't got any spare money to invest you can still invest your time and effort into refining your financial intelligence. There are many simple and inexpensive ways to begin to refine your financial thinking. It is your thoughts about your finances that will have a major impact on your situation.

A great place to start would be getting yourself a copy of "The Richest Man In Babylon" by George S. Clason. It is a simple story that will help you develop a plan to eliminate debt and to build a foundation allowing you to begin to invest, or in other words, get your money to work for you rather than you just working for money. The main message of the story is to pay yourself first. Ten percent of all the money you earn is yours to keep, and this 10 percent must be paid to yourself before you pay the bills or start buying stuff. This 10 percent can only be used in a way that causes it to grow and earn more money. It is not to be used for a holiday or to pay bills. This book has a very simple and very powerful message. Be sure to get it.

Another author I would recommend is Robert Kyosaki. He has created the "Rich Dad, Poor Dad" series of books. One of the ideas I have learned from him is his distinction of what is an asset and what is a liability. He basically says that an asset is something that puts money into your pocket and a liability is something that takes money out of your pocket.

Some of the most simple advice can be the most worthwhile. I remember attending a conference many years ago and one of the speakers was Tom Hopkins, a real estate coach, and he spoke about sales techniques. He also said he was going to share with us the most powerful bit of information about building wealth he had ever heard. He continued to tease us and build the drama about sharing this life-changing information with us throughout the speech. Eventually he wound up his speech and gave us his best financial advice, it was "Earn more than you spend." When he said that, the crowd erupted with laughter, but the silly thing is the majority of people don't take this very simple advice!

Special Bonus Offer

If you would like more information on the strategies, tools and techniques available to help you grow your business or you would just like to follow me on this journey:

Visit this page to access bonus content that will help you apply the concepts in the book:

http://bit.ly/1tQhLCA

CHAPTER 42

BEWARE, THE SOCIAL HYPNOSIS

Can you remember right back to chapter 1 when I first mentioned "Social Hypnosis"? Now I am going to go into more detail about it. I think Social Hypnosis is about how our attitudes and beliefs can be formed by being influenced by how others think. Everyone has certain beliefs and attitudes and when we ask ourselves for proof that these beliefs and attitudes are correct, often we can't find any.

I am not saying for one moment that they are wrong. I am simply saying that often we have no proof for some of the things we believe. We simply have adopted a belief because most of the people we are surrounded by believe the same thing. Why are you bringing this up? I hear you ask. Often we can prevent ourselves from learning quite valuable and life-changing ideas because our mind is closed off by our current beliefs. Social Hypnosis, in and of itself, is not a bad thing. In fact, having generalising beliefs allows us to function more effectively. Imagine having to explore all of the ramifications of every single decision that you make in your day, you would go crazy and get nothing done.

In the workshops I run I come across many people who are quite stressed about things. Quite often the way they interpret things is the cause of their stress. By simply changing their interpretation, the stress can disappear in an instant. But because they hang on to their way of thinking, "Because that's what everyone else thinks," nothing changes, and the stress continues to build. When it is suggested to them to change their thinking, they fight tooth-and-nail to hang on to the old belief simply because of the weight of numbers of people they know that believe the same thing.

I suggest that you should examine your beliefs and attitudes in the areas of your life that aren't going the way you would like them to. Then question their validity. A great question to explore is: "Is there a way of thinking about this that could give me a better outcome?"

Special Bonus Offer

If you would like more information on the strategies, tools and techniques available to help you grow your business or you would just like to follow me on this journey:

Visit this page to access bonus content that will help you apply the concepts in the book:

http://bit.ly/1tQhLCA

CHAPTER 43

THINGS DON'T JUST HAPPEN, THEY HAPPEN JUST

"Things don't just happen, they happen just." I heard this saying many years ago and I took a shine to it. And in most cases it is very true. I say in most cases, as there are occasions where people do have things happen that are unfair and unjust.

I am referring to the people who believe that life is unfair because life hasn't handed them everything on a silver platter with no effort. Examples of this are people who suffer from stress as a result of being under time pressure at work and at home. They are always rushing, complaining of not having time for themselves, always exhausted. The same people have never put any effort into learning how to plan, learning how to use a diary or a time management tool effectively. They have chosen to put no effort into clearly defining their goals and what really is important in their life. Other examples might be: people struggling financially as a result of not putting any effort into learning some fundamental financial intelligence, like I covered just a few chapters ago; and people who suffer ill health through totally preventable lifestyle choices, such as, drinking alcohol excessively, smoking, or taking drugs.

Imagine a world where everyone took personal responsibility for themselves and didn't blame their pain, illness, stress or financial situation on someone or something else. How simple is it to eat mostly living and live foods instead of taking the easy way out and consuming masses of processed foods? It is easy to drink 3 or 4 litres of water a day instead of coffee, tea, soft drinks and alcoholic drinks. And how about moving around a bit, instead of driving everywhere and always taking the lift.

This approach may seem harsh to some readers so I reiterate that I acknowledge that there are situations where some people are dealt a very unfair and unjust blow. I am simply focusing on the massive amount of physical, emotional and financial pain that so many people suffer that is totally preventable with a little bit of personal effort, study, practice and discipline.

I endeavor to see the abovementioned challenges as just that, challenges, and view them as signals that life is sending me to look more closely at myself, my knowledge and my skills, rather than looking for someone or something else to blame. Take this approach and things will begin to change for the better in ways you cannot imagine. It is a very simple idea but I didn't say it is easy!

CHAPTER 44

WE ALL NEED A REASON

I often get asked questions about how to do this and how can I get my self to do that. In many cases it is a matter of getting off your butt and doing things, instead of wasting energy trying to work out why you don't do certain things. Having said that I believe the process can be made a little easier by understanding that having a clear reason or benefit can cause us to change our habits and behaviours for the better.

For example, I am often asked, "Can you tell me why I just can't get out of bed in the morning?" or "After I get home from work I just can't get myself to exercise, I just want to sit on the lounge, why?" One of the answers is not having a clearly understood reason or benefit for doing those things. As many of you have experienced you don't have any trouble getting out of bed to get to the airport to catch the flight taking you on a holiday. And I am sure if your house was on fire you wouldn't have any trouble finding the energy to get up and run. Both of these scenarios have one thing in common, a reason and a benefit.

If you want to change some of your habits and behaviours I suggest you put some time, energy and effort into looking for and getting clear about the reason and benefits of the new habit or behaviour. I have explained this to some people in the past, and when I checked back in with them after some time had elapsed and asked how they were progressing, I was told that they couldn't find the time or energy to do the work to find reasons and benefits! There is a limit for me to be able to help some people. At some stage people need to take responsibility for how their lives turn out. For anyone to benefit from this idea they will need to decide to put in the effort. That effort will be rewarded.

I am assuming that because you are still reading this that you have picked up the mantle of personal responsibility and you are willing to take action to improve the bits of your life that you want to improve, you just need some guidance and information. So go ahead and identify some areas you want to improve, get clear, very clear, on the reasons and benefits for the change, work out a plan of attack and then attack the plan!

Special Bonus Offer

If you would like more information on the strategies, tools and techniques available to help you grow your business or you would just like to follow me on this journey:

Visit this page to access bonus content that will help you apply the concepts in the book:

http://bit.ly/1tQhLCA

CHAPTER 45

IT'S YOUR CHOICE

It is amazing how often I get into conversations with people and the subject ends up being "choice". Whenever I do personal coaching or run a seminar, I find getting people to buy into the idea that there is always a choice in life, seems to be the most difficult.

I personally believe that we have choice in everything we do. When I explain this it is common for someone to interpret it in a way that gets them saying "No" to everything in life that they dislike. Let me explain. If someone says to me, "I have to go to work tomorrow" I challenge them and say, "You are actually choosing to go to work tomorrow." This usually gets the response, "Well if I don't go to work I will lose my job." This is probably true, so it would be a silly choice to make, but it is a choice, go to work or lose your job. There are options making it a choice.

The point of the whole conversation is to help people understand that almost everything works out better if you make it a choice. Some examples I hear of people giving away control is when they say things like, "I don't have time to...", "I have to...", "I can't...". There are many ways of giving away control and my suggestion is to identify them and destroy them. The culmination of continuously giving away control in these seemingly insignificant ways is the loss of control over your life's direction and your emotional experience.

Instead of saying, "I don't have time to..." say "I choose not to...". Instead of saying "I have to..." say "I choose to...". Instead of saying, "I can't" use the word "won't", the outcome is the same for both, but one puts you in control, the other takes control away. The bottom line is that you will feel, perform and produce in a more positive way by choosing your actions rather than being a victim about it.

I have found by telling yourself the truth it can change your action in a positive and profound way. You are the worst person to lie to. This falls under the category of simple but not easy. When you take back control with your words, the benefits will be many. Someone once challenged me with this question, "There are results and excuses, which one are you?" It is a very thought-provoking question and it takes away the safety net of excuses that we use to protect ourselves when we don't do what we know we should. When we make a choice we also choose the consequences, and when we don't choose, we must own the consequences of our choice not to choose.

Special Bonus Offer
Visit this page to access bonus content that will help you apply the concepts in the book:
http://bit.ly/1tQhLCA

CHAPTER 46

YOU GET WHAT YOU EXPECT, SOMETIMES!

Many people get bent out of shape when things don't go the way they want them to. I think it is great to have very high expectations of yourself, but as the old saying goes, "Be careful of what you expect, because you might just get it."

There are a couple of points I would like to share in this chapter, the first is, be a bit kind to yourself and look at the big picture. We often get upset when things don't go our way but we need to look at this in the context of the "whole deal". "Pistol" Pete Sampras is one of the legends of the game of tennis. He won 73 percent of the matches he played in his professional career. This meant that he lost roughly a little under a third of the time. We have, in Australia, Leigh Matthews, who I have spoken about before. Leigh is a legend of our game of AFL (Australian Football League). As both a player and now a coach, Leigh's statistics are such that he won 68 percent of the games that he was involved in as either a player or a coach.

What does all this mean? Well the way I think about it is that if the legends of their chosen field only win around 60 to 70 percent of the time, we really need to understand that with us "mere mortals", things won't always go our way, so we need to give ourselves a bit of consideration in that area. This does not mean that you should lower your expectations by any stretch of the imagination, in fact I have heard Leigh say that he doesn't know of anything that will guarantee success, but he knows of plenty of things that will guarantee failure. I think having low expectations is one of those things that will guarantee failure.

You must have high expectations but you must also know that the setbacks and losses are there for you to learn and grow from, they are not there for you to get frustrated and give up over. So set the bar high and focus on the process and the things you have control over. Prepare everything you can to the highest standard that you are aware of currently, continue to learn and the results will be what they will be.

Special Bonus Offer

If you would like more information on the strategies, tools and techniques available to help you grow your business or you would just like to follow me on this journey:

Visit this page to access bonus content that will help you apply the concepts in the book:

http://bit.ly/1tQhLCA

CHAPTER 47

USE WHAT YOU ALREADY HAVE

There is an incredible number of people I see that have challenges in their life and have the skills and ability to overcome these challenges, but don't use them. I know many performers, actors and athletes that have amazing skills, which they use in their professional lives and yet never think to use in their personal lives. I have met actors who have the skill to manage their emotional state under incredible pressure for their profession, but lose it completely in their personal lives. I have worked with athletes who have a sensational ability to handle pressure situations in their sporting lives but crumble under much less pressure personally.

In your case, I am sure that you have skills and abilities that you use in certain areas of your life that can be used in other areas. It is just that perhaps you don't think about it. For example, you might be terrific at riding a mountain bike; you are confident, you have good balance and you feel very comfortable dodging and weaving around trees and obstacles. However, when it comes time to speak in public, you go weak in the knees and break out in a sweat. If you take the time to identify the way you speak to yourself, how you picture yourself and what sort of body language you use when thinking or talking about mountain bike riding and begin to consciously use the same self-talk, visualisation and body language in relation to public speaking, you will find that your experience will change.

This is a very simple process that will work for just about anything. Again, I said simple not easy. It is one of those things that I often talk about that are simple yet challenging, but always worth the effort.

Special Bonus Offer

If you would like more information on the strategies, tools and techniques available to help you grow your business or you would just like to follow me on this journey:

Visit this page to access bonus content that will help you apply the concepts in the book:

http://bit.ly/1tQhLCA

CHAPTER 48

BECOME A LIFE-LONG LEARNER

One of the most magnificent things in life, I think, is learning. Learning anything! Just fall in love with learning, get curious. There is so much information and so many ideas out there it is amazing. I am mentioning this because in my observations I see so many people just doing, thinking and experiencing the same things day after week after month, and it seems that many of them have lost the desire to learn anything new. They are so caught up being busy, that they miss out on all the amazing opportunities that life can provide.

Of course, I continue to learn heaps from a professional perspective, in some cases through necessity, but mostly through curiosity, and I love it! But on the personal side, I just love learning about different things. Over the years I have been an electrician, a salesman, a photocopier technician, a professional musician and many other twists and turns have been taken. Most recently I have developed an interest in motorcycle riding and in the last year I have done at least five different courses. I have just started scuba diving in the last couple of years and continue to do courses to refine my skills and knowledge. I go four wheel driving and have done courses about it. I have a passion for sailing and I am constantly learning about it. I have invested loads of time and money in learning about computers, software, hardware, flying helicopters, doing woodwork, welding, building, photography, audiovisual stuff and the list just keeps going on and on.

My point is that constant and never-ending improvement is essential, because if you are not green and growing then you are ripe and rotting! I am sure that there are many things that you would love to learn more about or experience, so I am suggesting that you ensure that your daily, weekly and monthly planning creates the space for you to get into it. As you have probably heard, you don't get a rehearsal for life — this is it. So don't waste a second of it, get out there. Experience and learn as much as you can.

Just look at people like Albert Schweitzer who was a world-renowned concert organist, an M.D., a surgeon, a missionary, an author, a teacher, a theologian, a pastor, a philosopher, and he established and ran a hospital, and the list goes on. It is reported that he slept no more than three hours a night from the age of 17. He died in 1965 at the age of 90. He won the Nobel Peace Prize in 1952 for his efforts. I think Albert used every moment of his life to the fullest, how are you doing?

CHAPTER 49

THE LAST WORD

Congratulations for getting all the way through the book. This is the final chapter. I sure hope you have gained some value from reading my book.

I would encourage you to read and re-read parts of this book that are relevant to what challenges you are facing or goals you want to achieve at any given time.

I am sure you have heard the saying "knowledge is power", well I tend to disagree. I really believe the answer is in the doing, the action. So the saying should really be "Applied knowledge is power. We use a saying in our business that we borrowed from somewhere many years ago, "the difference between doing it and not doing it, is doing it"

It has been fun thinking about all of the chapter topics and the remembering the details and stories. At times I found writing this challenging, as my mind would go blank.

I would like to thank all of the people that sent questions to me through my website and particularly those who took the time to send me their wonderful stories.

If I had one last thing to say that would blow your mind this is where I would have written it!

Special Bonus Offer

If you would like more information on the strategies, tools and techniques available to help you grow your business or you would just like to follow me on this journey:

Visit this page to access bonus content that will help you apply the concepts in the book:

http://bit.ly/1tQhLCA

I'm nowhere near as good as I'm going to get

"Don't expect Mick to fix you up in one day. In my experience you'll get the tools to fix yourself over time. Repetition, repetition and more repetition is the key. I'm a lot better than I was in all important areas of my life, though I'm nowhere near as good as I'm going to get."

George W Wilson — Finance and Administration Manager, Colony 47 Inc

This has resulted in vast improvement

"We have found Mick's programs to be very effective, by empowering our people to succeed during challenging times that our industry has been facing. This has resulted in vast improvements in the sense of team, increased levels of enthusiasm, and improved morale. We would recommend Mick's programs to any individual or business which is serious about positive change."

Greg Jones — State Operations Manager, Cripps Nubake

It has helped me tremendously

"I continue to refine and refresh what is taught in Mick's programs. It has helped me tremendously and helped me to work with my team. The good input I have received from the programs has enabled me to help others as well as myself."

Wayne Bailey — The Mercury Newspaper

The benefits are huge

"The list of positive changes in our lives goes on and on and the benefits are huge. I am going on a 6km fun run this weekend — 3 months ago I didn't have enough energy to walk up the hill."

Suzzane Purdon

THANK YOU

"I cannot thank you guys for all the help in the last year.
THANK YOU, THANK YOU,
THANK YOU AGAIN AND AGAIN."

Beverly Challenger — PRD Nationwide Real Estate

ATTENTION: SERIOUS READERS!

If you have made it this far through the book I know you are a serious student.

So I have prepared some VERY SPECIAL just for you.

Just Visit:
www.uncoverhiddenprofits.com

Go there right now and you will find exactly what you need to continue your awesome personal development journey.

Mick Hawes

PS. If you have read this book you know that procrastination is the biggest time and life thief on the planet, so don't let this criminal control you, go and check out this VERY SPECIAL offer right now!
www.uncoverhiddenprofits.com

PPS. You shouldn't still be reading this, go here now!

www.uncoverhiddenprofits.com